MW01115419

Computers and Information Processing: Concepts and Applications

Sixth Edition

Steven L. Mandell
Bowling Green State University

West Publishing Company
St. Paul   New York   Los Angeles   San Francisco

WEST'S COMMITMENT TO THE ENVIRONMENT

In 1906, West Publishing Company began recycling materials left over from the production of books. This began a tradition of efficient and responsible use of resources. Today, up to 95% of our legal books and 70% of our college texts are printed on recycled, acid-free stock. West also recycles nearly 22 million pounds of scrap paper annually—the equivalent of 181,717 trees. Since the 1960s, West has devised ways to capture and recycle waste inks, solvents, oils, and vapors created in the printing process. We also recycle plastics of all kinds, wood, glass, corrugated cardboard, and batteries, and have eliminated the use of styrofoam book packaging. We at West are proud of the longevity and the scope of our commitment to our environment.

Production, Prepress, Printing and Binding by West Publishing Company.

Contents

Introduction

This study guide has been designed to accompany *Computers and Information Processing, Concepts and Applications*, 6th edition, published by West Publishing Company. Throughout its development, emphasis has been placed on providing a vehicle that can assist the student in learning the text material. No design will ever take the place of conscientious student effort; however, the approaches incorporated within this study guide will make the task less difficult.

The structure of the study guide parallels the textbook. Within each chapter the student will encounter distinct segments. A list of KEY TERMS with definitions is provided at the beginning to orient the student toward the important concepts covered in the text. Following the key terms is a chapter SUMMARY. A series of multiple choice questions with explanatory answers has been formatted into a STRUCTURED LEARNING environment. Utilizing this technique, the student can "walk through" the material in a progressive fashion. TRUE/FALSE and MATCHING questions permit the student to obtain immediate feedback on comprehension. SHORT ANSWER exercises provide the student with an opportunity to express an understanding of the material. Solutions to the problems are presented in an ANSWER KEY so that the student can evalutate and diagnose progress. Solutions to the problems are presented in an ANSWER KEY at the end of the study guide.

The BASIC supplement to the study guide is designed to support the BASIC programming supplement in *Computers and Informationn Processing, Concepts and Applications, with BASIC*. The section structure also parallels the text material; however, a slightly different format is utilized. A scaled-down version of STRUCTURED LEARNING is presented initially as a review mechanism. A WORKSHEET is then provided for the student to apply programming concepts and techniques. Two PROGRAMMING PROBLEMS are presented as the ultimate evaluation exercise for each section. The solutions for the odd-numbered problems are incorporated into the ANSWER KEY at the end of the study guide, and the solutions for the even-numbered problems are presented in the Instructor's Manual.

Good Luck!

Steven L. Mandell

CHAPTER 1

Introduction to Information Processing

❏ KEY TERMS

Access   To get, or retrieve, data from a computer system.

Analog computer   A computer that measures the change in continuous electrical or physical conditions rather than counting data; contrast with digital computer.

Bit (BInary digiT)   The smallest unit of data that the computer can handle and that can be represented in the digits 0 and 1 of binary notation.

Byte   A fixed number of adjacent bits operated on as a unit.

Central processing unit (CPU)   Acts as the "brain" of the computer; composed of three sections—arithmetic/logic unit (ALU), control unit, and memory unit.

Character   A letter, number, or symbol (such as %, #, or !). Characters are represented by bytes in computer systems.

Computer   A general-purpose electronic machine with applications limited only by the creativity of the humans who use it; its power is derived from its speed, accuracy, and memory.

Data   Facts; the raw material of information.

Data base   Collection of data that is commonly defined and consistently organized to fit the information needs of a wide variety of users in an organization.

Data processing   The steps involved in collecting, manipulating, and distributing data.

Digital computer   Type of computer that operates on distinct data (for example, digits) by performing arithmetic and logic processes on specific data units.

Electronic data processing (EDP)   Data processing performed largely by electronic equipment, such as computers, rather than by manual or mechanical methods.

Feedback   A check within a system to see if predetermined goals are being met; determines the effectiveness of a system.

Field   A meaningful group of characters, such as a social security number or a person's name.

File   A grouping of related records, such as student records; sometimes referred to as a data set.

Hard copy   Printed output.

Hardware   Physical components that make up a computer system.

Information   Data that has been organized and processed so that it is meaningful.

Information processing   The conversion of data to information.

Input   Data submitted to the computer for processing.

Mainframe   A large, full-scale computer that can support many peripherals and many users.

Memory   The section of the computer that holds instructions, data, and intermediate and final results during processing; also known as internal memory, primary memory, and main memory.

Microcomputer   A smaller, low-priced computer used in homes, schools, and businesses; also called a personal or home computer.

Microprocessor   A programmable processing unit (placed on a silicon chip) containing arithmetic, logic, and control circuitry; used in microcomputers, calculators, microwave ovens, and many other applications.

Minicomputer   A computer with the components of a full-sized system but with a smaller memory capacity.

Office automation   Integration of computer and communication technology with traditional office procedures to increase productivity and efficiency.

Output   Information that comes from the computer, as a result of processing, into a form that can be used by people.

Packaged software   Standardized, commercial software, with procedures and documentation, developed for solving a wide variety of specific problems.

Peripheral devices   Device that attaches to the central processing unit, such as a storage device or an input or output device.

Processing   The stage of the data processing flow that occurs in a computer's CPU and includes classifying, sorting, calculating, summarizing, and storing.

Program   The instructions issued to the computer so that specific tasks may be completed; also called software.

Programming language   A communication system, or code, that people can use to communicate with computers.

Record   A collection of data items, or fields, that relates to a single unit, such as a student.

Soft copy   A temporary, or nonpermanent, record of machine output such as a CRT display.

Software   Program or programs used to direct the computer in solving problems and overseeing operations.

Storage   Holding place that exists on media such as disks or tapes and supplements CPU memory; is external to the CPU and thus data is accessed at slower speeds than from memory; also referred to as secondary, external, or auxiliary storage.

Supercomputer   The largest, fastest, most expensive type of computer in existence, capable of performing millions of calculations per second and processing enormous amounts of data.

❑ SUMMARY

The two main parts of a computer are hardware, the tangible components of the computer, and software (or programs), the instructions that tell the computer what it is to do. Hardware includes the computer and also peripheral devices such as printers and storage devices.

Data processing involves collecting, manipulating, and distributing data to achieve certain goals. The use of computers in data processing is called electronic data processing (EDP). Data processing is not the same as information processing. Information processing is all the steps in converting data to information. Data, the raw facts gathered from various sources but not organized in a meaningful way, cannot be used to make meaningful decisions. Information is processed data that increases understanding and helps people make intelligent decisions.

Data should be organized in an integrated way. Data items range from the smallest unit, the bit, to the largest, the data base. A bit (binary digit) is the 0 or 1 used to represent the on/off states of electrical circuitry. A character (letter, number, or symbol) is represented by combinations of bits, or a byte. A field is a collection of related characters that convey a unit of information. A collection of fields that relate to a single unit is a record. A grouping of related records is a file. A method of structuring data is called a data base.

All processing has the same basic flow: input, processing, and output. Input is the action of collecting data and converting it to computer readable form. The three input steps are collecting, verifying, and coding.

Processing occurs in the central processing unit (CPU). The CPU includes circuitry for arithmetic and logical operations and memory. Processing includes classifying, sorting, calculating, summarizing, and storing data.

Output is information that comes from processing and is distributed to users. The two types of output are soft copy (temporary) and hard copy (tangible). Three steps are necessary for output: retrieving, converting, and communicating information. Feedback is the process of evaluating the output and making adjustments to ensure that information does not lose its value for decision making.

A computer depends on human intelligence and directions. It has only three functions: arithmetic operations, logical comparisons of relationships among values, and storage and retrieval operations. The computer has three advantages over the human brain: its speed (millions of operations in one second), its accuracy (the inherent reliability of circuitry), and its storage capacity.

Analog computers measure changes in continuous physical or electrical states. Digital computers, which this text discusses, count in discrete on/off states, represented by binary digits.

A microcomputer, or personal computer, contains a microprocessor—a chip that is etched with many circuits. The chip contains the parts of a CPU that control the arithmetic and logic operations, and possibly some memory. Software for microcomputers is often packaged, but many users write their own. Minicomputers vary in size from desktop to file cabinet size. They use standard electrical outlets. No air conditioning is required and standardized packaged software is available. Mainframes operate at very high speeds and handle other high speed equipment. They require special platforms and special electrical wiring. Mainframe vendors typically offer a great deal of support. Supercomputers are the fastest and most expensive type of computer. They need liquid coolant around their chips to prevent melting. They are used for lengthy and complex calculations.

Originally, computers were used primarily by scientists, mathematicians, and engineers. Today, computers are available in many forms for numerous purposes. Computers are widely used in business, including banking, manufacturing, management, and office automation functions; education; medicine; government; and general home use. Computer-based training (CBT) and multimedia configurations will change education and industry in the future.

❏ STRUCTURED LEARNING

1. For effective processing, data is organized in the following manner: _____.
   a. classify, sort, calculate, summarize, store
   b. input, processing, output, feedback
   c. bit, character, field, record, file, data base
   d. data, information

c. Data is organized in a hierarchy from the smallest unit a computer can handle, the bit, to the largest unit of organization, the data base.

2. The objective of all data processing is _____.
   a. the conversion of data into information that can be used in making decisions
   b. to accumulate as much data as possible in the smallest possible area
   c. to convert all manual systems to automated in order to eliminate human error
   d. to make data easy to store and retrieve when the data is needed

a. Data processing refers to collecting, manipulating, and distributing data to achieve certain goals. Data not organized or defined in a meaningful manner cannot be used to make valid decisions.

3. The steps collect, verify, and code constitute the _____ stage of the data flow.
   a. feedback
   b. output
   c. processing
   d. input

d. Before processing can occur, data must be input. The data must be gathered, verified for accuracy, and put into a form the computer can understand.

4. The phrase garbage in, garbage out is most descriptive of the activities that occur in the _____ stage of the data flow.
   a. output
   b. input
   c. processing
   d. feedback

b. Because input involves collecting and verifying data, it is the stage at which accuracy is crucial for output to be meaningful. A case could be made for feedback as the correct answer, because it is here that GIGO problems are often uncovered; this, however, occurs after the fact, thus b is the correct answer.

5. Physical factors affecting computer speed are the _____.
   a. size of the diskette and the voltage from the electrical outlet
   b. switching speed of electrical components and the distance electrical currents must travel
   c. number of peripheral devices used and the typing speed of the user
   d. speed of light and the amount of air conditioning required

---

b. Electrical current moves at a constant speed, so the switching speed and distance the current must travel determine the computer's speed. Other factors include program language, amount of data the computer can handle, and amount of data and instructions available.

6. The term digital describes the type of computer being discussed in the text because _____.
   a. in these computers, data is represented by discrete on/off states
   b. these computers measure changes in continuous physical or electrical states
   c. these computers use electricity
   d. digital computers rely on memory for their operations

---

a. Digital computers count in discrete units.

7. The type of computers usually used as single-user systems are _____.
   a. minicomputers   c. supercomputers
   b. microcomputers   d. mainframes

---

b. Because of the limits of memory and the fact that each has its own CPU, most microcomputers are used by one user each, although they can be linked to networks.

---

8. Supercomputers are normally used for _____.
   a. figuring lengthy and complex calculations   c. running packaged software programs
   b. everyday business operations   d. financial calculations

---

a. Supercomputers are used in fields where enormous amounts of data are processed at once. These include weather forecasting, nuclear reactor safety analysis, and stress tests in auto and aircraft design.

9. Applications such as word processing, information retrieval, electronic mail, and telecommuting are part of the general computer application _____.
    a. computer-based training
    b. multimedia
    c. office automation
    d. synthesis

---

c. The term office automation describes the integration of computer and communication technology such as word processing and e-mail with traditional office procedures.

10. The largest user of computers in the U.S. is _____.
    a. IBM
    b. General Motors
    c. the federal government
    d. elementary schools

---

c. The federal government agencies are involved in storing and processing information for the census, income tax, Library of Congress, FBI, and the welfare and social security systems.

❏ TRUE/FALSE

1. T F A machine becomes a computer when it contains memory. F

2. T F Analog computers are less accurate than digital computers.

3. T F For most of us, computers are remote and have little effect on our lives. F

4. T F Data is processed information that increases understanding and helps people make decisions.

5. T F Packaged software is standardized, commercial software developed for solving general problems.

6. T F Once the data flow stages are designed and set up, it is no longer necessary to monitor them by feedback. F

7. T F The character (byte) is the smallest unit of data. F

8. T F Input includes both the data that is to be manipulated and the software.

9. T F Soft-copy output is information that has been printed on paper. F

10. T F Data stored in memory can be accessed repeatedly unless replaced or overwritten by new data.

❏ MATCHING

a. hardware   f. storage

b. byte   g. retrieval

c. file   h. field

d. microprocessor   i. soft copy

e. analog   j. microcomputer

1. The tangible parts of a computer, are known as _____.

2. Temporary output seen on a monitor is called _____.

3. Places that are external to the computer and used for holding data are called _____.

4. Computers that measure changes in continuous physical or electrical states are _____ computers.

5. Getting data from storage is called _____.

6. A chip that contains the parts of the CPU that control the computer and perform arithmetic and logic operations is called the _____.

7. Another name for the personal computer is the _____.

8. The group of bits that represents a character is the _____.

9. A group of related records is a(n) _____.

10. Related characters making up a unit of information are known as a(n) _____.

❏ SHORT ANSWER

1. Name the three steps all processing follows.

   Input, processing output

2. Describe the difference between an analog computer and a digital computer.

chg in electrical or physical conditions

on/off switches

3. What are the three basic functions of a computer?

arithmetic
storage/retrieval
logical comparison

4. Describe the class of supercomputers.

largest
fastest
most expensive

5. How are computers used in education?

CBT

6. Describe the three steps in data output.

retrieving
converting
proper time/use/people

7. What is the purpose of the CPU?

handles processing
- arithmetic
- logical comp
- primary memory

8. What current trend is evident in the use of minicomputers and microcomputers?

   micros are becoming more powerful
   + used 4 mainframes.

9. What is information processing?

   Steps involved in converting data into information

10. How is feedback helpful in information processing?

    To ensure processing results in good information

CHAPTER 2

The Evolution of Computers

❏ KEY TERMS

Abacus A rectangular frame with beads strung on wires and used for calculating.

Accounting machine A mechanically operated forerunner of the computer; could read data from punched cards, do calculations, rearrange data, and print results in varied formats.

Analytical engine A machine designed by Charles Babbage for doing calculations and storing results in a memory unit; too advanced for the technology of its time, it was forgotten for nearly one hundred years.

Artificial intelligence (AI) A field of research developing techniques to use computers for solving problems that appear to require imagination, intuition, or intelligence.

Bletchley Park Computer A computer built by two Englishmen, Dilwyn Knox and Alan Turing, that was used successfully during World War II for deciphering German codes.

EDVAC (Electronic Discrete Variable Automatic Computer) A stored-program computer developed at the University of Pennsylvania.

ENIAC (Electronic Numerical Integrator and Calculator) The first general-purpose electronic digital computer; it was developed by John W. Mauchly and J. Presper Eckert Jr. at the University of Pennsylvania.

First-generation computer A computer that used vacuum tubes and was much faster than mechanical devices, but very slow in comparison to today's computer; developed in the 1950s.

Fourth-generation computer A computer that uses chips made by large-scale integration and offers significant price and performance improvements over earlier computers.

Integrated circuit (IC) An electronic circuit etched on a tiny silicon chip, enabling much faster processing than transistors and at a greatly reduced price.

Large-scale integration (LSI) A method by which circuits containing thousands of electronic components are densely packed on a single silicon chip.

Machine language The only set of instructions that a computer can execute directly; a code that designates the proper electrical states in the computer as combinations of 0s and 1s.

Magnetic core Iron-alloy, doughnut-shaped ring about the size of a pinhead of which memory is built; one core stores one binary digit (its state is determined by the direction of an electrical current); the cores are strung on a grid of fine wires that carry the current.

Magnetic drum Cylinder with a magnetic outer surface on which data can be stored by magnetizing specific positions on the surface.

Mark I The first automatic calculator.

Napier's Bones A portable multiplication tool designed by John Napier consisting of ivory rods that are slid up and down against each other; forerunner of the slide rule.

Pascaline A device invented by Blaise Pascal used to add and subtract; a series of rotating gears performed the calculations.

Punched card A heavy paper storage medium on which data is represented by holes punched according to a coding scheme much like that used on Hollerith's cards.

Remote terminal A terminal located some distance (in another room or building or another town, state, or country) from the main computer and linked to it through cables and phone lines.

Second-generation computer A computer that used transistors; it was smaller, faster, and had a larger memory capacity than first-generation computers.

Stepped Reckoner Machine designed by von Leibniz that could add, subtract, multiply, divide, and calculate square roots.

Stored-program concept The idea that program instructions can be stored in memory in electrical form so that no human intervention is required during processing and so that the computer can process the instructions at its own speed.

Symbolic language The use of mnemonic symbols to represent instructions; must be translated into machine language before being executed by the computer.

Third-generation computer A computer characterized by the use of integrated circuits, reduced size, lower costs, and increased speed and reliability.

Transistor Type of solid state circuitry used in second-generation computers; smaller, faster, and more reliable than vacuum tubes but inferior to third-generation, large-scale integration.

UNIVAC I (UNIVersal Automatic Computer)   One of the first commercial electronic computers; generally used for business applications; became available in 1951.

Vacuum tube   A glass device (resembling a light bulb) from which almost all air has been removed and through which electricity passes; often found in old radios and televisions; used in first-generation computers for controlling internal operations.

Very-large-scale integration (VLSI)   A type of circuitry replacing large-scale integration in fourth-generation computers; smaller, faster, and less costly than LSI circuitry.

❑ SUMMARY

The computer has only become reality in the last few decades, but the theories and ideas on which it is based can be traced back through the centuries. Computer technology has passed through four stages called generations, each of which is marked by a significant development.

The abacus, with its beads and wires, was one of the earliest calculating tools. In the early 1600s, John Napier invented Napier's Bones, a device made of ivory rods that could be used to multiply and divide. Napier's Bones were the forerunners of the slide rule. Two other calculating tools were invented but not widely used in the mid- to late-1600s. The first was the Pascaline, designed by Blaise Pascal. It could be used for adding and subtracting, but was unacceptable to accountants who feared the loss of their jobs. The second was the Stepped Reckoner, developed by Gottfried Wilhelm von Leibniz for adding, subtracting, multiplying, dividing, and square roots. Almost every mechanical calculator built during the next 150 years was based on its design.

The next major development occurred in the weaving industry when Joseph Jacquard invented a loom that was programmed with punched cards. The loom demonstrated that information could be coded on punched cards; cards could be linked in series, or program; and jobs could be automated. Charles Babbage, the father of computers, was the first person to apply the concepts demonstrated in Jacquard's loom to calculating machines. Babbage envisioned a machine, the analytical engine, that was amazingly similar to modern computers.

Dr. Herman Hollerith invented a machine that read and compiled data from punched cards to tabulate the U.S. census. Hollerith sold his company, the Tabulating Machine Company, and it later became IBM under Thomas Watson in 1924. The IBM machines used updated forms of the punched card. Accounting machines that manipulated vast quantities of these cards were used in business until well into the 1950s.

War time engendered computing machines for specific war-time needs, such as breaking codes, calculating trajectories, and designing weapons. The Bletchley Park computer, developed by Dilwyn Knox and Alan Turing, was successfully used for deciphering codes churned out by the German Enigma machine. The Mark I, the first automatic calculator, was designed by Howard Aiken's team at Harvard and was used for weapons design and trajectories.

The shift from mechanically-oriented machines to those using electronic parts was demonstrated by the ENIAC, designed by John Mauchly and J. Presper Eckert, Jr. at the University of Pennsylvania. The ENIAC's major problem was that humans were needed to set switches and connect wires on control panels called plugboards each time a different program was used. John von Neumann worked on the notion of the stored program in which instructions would be put in memory. Stored programs led to the building of EDVAC and the beginning of the modern computer era.

The first generation of computers used the ENIAC and EDVAC design. The first commercial electronic computer, the UNIVAC I, took IBM's place at the census bureau. These computers used vacuum tubes, were coded in machine language, stored data on magnetic drums, and frequently broke down. During this time, symbolic languages with mnemonic symbols were written to minimize errors in coding. Grace Murray Hopper helped write language-translator programs that made high-level languages possible.

The second-generation computers were characterized by four hardware advances: transistors, magnetic-core memory, magnetic tapes, and magnetic disks. The use of magnetic cores facilitated real-time processing.

Third-generation computers, characterized by integrated circuits (ICs), used less power, cost less, and were smaller and more reliable than previous machines.

Fourth-generation computers are characterized by memory on silicon chips. Placing large numbers of circuits on a single chip is called large-scale integration (LSI). LSI is being replaced by very-large-scale integration (VLSI). The development of the computer on a chip, or microprocessor, during the fourth generation, has instigated another computer revolution, the use of microcomputers.

Originally, computer firms produced both hardware and software. Today there are many hardware manufacturers in existence. A 1969 court ruling forced IBM to "unbundle" its software—that is, sell its software separately from the hardware. A new industry consisting of independent software companies quickly became reality. These companies produced both specialty and generic programs.

Microcomputers and software for microcomputers have become the most popular type of computer. The microcomputer would not have been possible without the development of the microprocessor, a single chip containing arithmetic and logic circuitry and control capability for input and output access. The chip was designed by Ted Hoff of Intel Corp., for use in a calculator. Hoff's chip could manipulate 4-bits of data. By 1974, bit size increased to 8-bits, and the first microcomputers, among them the MITS Altair 8800 and the Apple II, were introduced. Many microcomputer companies following suit, including IBM, Commodore, and Tandy. Some companies have ceased to exist, but microcomputer use continues to increase as the chips become more powerful and less expensive, using 16-bit and 32-bit configurations.

1. The Electronic Numerical Integrator and Calculator (ENIAC) _____.
    a. handled most business processing until the 1950s
    b. was the first general-purpose machine to depend upon electronic components rather than electromechanical gears
    c. was designed by John von Neumann
    d. was the first commercial electronic computer

___

b. ENIAC was designed by Mauchly and Eckert at the University of Pennsylvania. It was the first electronic computer for large-scale general use.

2. What development really marked the beginning of the modern computer era and the information society?
    a. the stored-program concept
    b. the use vacuum-tubes and other electronic components
    c. the use of punched cards and punched tapes
    d. the development of binary numbers

___

a. The stored-program concept was devised by John von Neumann and incorporated into the EDVAC. This reduced the number of manual operations needed for computer processing, thus marking the beginning of automated computing.

___

3. The primary drawback of first-generation computers was that _____.
    a. they contained too many mechanical components
    b. they required manual switch setting and other manual preparations for running each different program
    c. they contained vacuum tubes that failed frequently
    d. computer firms could not build enough machines to meet the demand

___

c. UNIVAC I and others were huge, costly to buy, expensive to operate, and unreliable. The vacuum tubes produced too much heat and a tube would fail about every 15 minutes.

4. Fourth-generation computers began when _____.
   a. voice synthesis was invented
   b. magnetic cores were replaced by memory on silicon chips
   c. artificial intelligence (AI) became a practicality
   d. high-level languages were written

---

b. The beginning of fourth-generation computers is not clear-cut, but historians credit the silicon chip as being the dividing point.

5. Ironically, the miniaturization of integrated circuits led to _____.
   a. profit losses for computer manufacturers   c. the development of magnetic drums
   b. less memory space   d. supercomputers

---

d. By reducing the size of circuitry and changing the design of the chips, supercomputers were designed with memories large enough for complex calculations used in research and design.

6. Jacquard's loom is mentioned as important to the development of computers because _____.
   a. it was controlled by one of the early computers
   b. Charles Babbage studied Jacquard's ideas
   c. it was controlled by a "program" recorded on punched cards
   d. Jacquard received credit for his invention

---

c. Although Babbage did study Jacquard's ideas, the loom was important because it showed how punched cards could automate, or program, weaving to eliminate human skill.

7. The Whirlwind I was important for _____.
   a. its flight simulator   c. transistors
   b. real-time processing   d. business uses

---

b. The Whirlwind's capability for real-time processing was what enabled scientists to use it for flight simulation.

8. The emergence of the software industry is attributed largely to _____.
    a. a court decision forcing IBM to unbundle its software
    b. the development of high-level languages
    c. the growth of the hardware industry
    d. the introduction of VisiCalc

---

a. When IBM was forced to offer hardware and software for sale separately, this enabled small software developers to begin creating software, knowing that the success of selling software wouldn't be tied to the sale of a computer.

9. Babbage is known as the father of computers because _____.
    a. he built the Stepped Reckoner, which could add, subtract, multiply, divide, and figure square roots
    b. his loom used punched cards to store coded information
    c. his analytical machine had the four essential parts of a modern computer
    d. he formed the Tabulating Machine Company, which later became IBM

---

c. The parts could calculate, store instructions and results, carry out instructions, and read and write data to punched cards.

10. Integrated circuits are _____.
    a. components of electronic circuits placed together onto small silicon chips
    b. recognized as the beginning of fourth-generation computers
    c. transistors linked on circuit boards to form a larger memory
    d. 64 complete circuits on a silicon chip

---

a. A single silicon chip could hold thousands of electronic components.

❏ TRUE/FALSE

1. T F   The abacus was an early form of the slide rule.   F

2. T F   Herman Hollerith's machine was the first implementation of punched cards.   F

3. T F   The Mark I consisted of 78 accounting machines controlled by punched paper tapes.

4. T F   Fifth-generation computers are distinguished by memory on silicon chips.   F

5. T F Off-the-shelf software are generally more cost effective than custom-written programs.

6. T F There was little demand for Pascal's machine, the Pascaline, because clerks and accountants were afraid it would replace them at their jobs.

7. T F Very-large-scale-integration puts thousands of electrical components on a single silicon chip.

8. T F A law suit gave Mauchly and Eckert credit for the concepts used in the first electronic computer.

9. T F One major problem of ENIAC was that instructions had to be fed into it manually by setting switches and connecting wires on control panels.

10. T F Magnetic cores replaced magnetic drums as internal memory on third-generation computers.

❑ MATCHING

a. magnetic drums
b. Stepped Reckoner
c. Hollerith
d. microprocessor
e. Pascaline

f. analytical engine
g. Napier's Bones
h. VisiCalc
i. family
j. chip

1. The forerunner of the slide rule, which was invented in the mid-1600s, was _____.

2. Because a better method was needed for calculating tax reports, a Frenchman invented the _____.

3. Almost every mechanical calculator built from about 1700 to about 1850 was based on the design of the _____.

4. The first electronic spreadsheet for microcomputers was _____.

5. When IBM realized it was turning out too many incompatible machines, it introduced the concept of computers.

6. Babbage's ideas for the _____ were amazingly similar to the design of computers.

7. A machine that reduced the time it took to compile census data from seven and one-half years to two and one-half years was developed by _____.

a 8. Cylinders coated with magnetizable material and used for storage are _____.

d 9. Another name for a "computer on a chip" is _____.

j 10. The _____ marked the beginning of third-generation computers.

❑ SHORT ANSWER

1. What problem of first-generation computers has reappeared in supercomputers?

heat

2. Even in the 1600s, what kinds of problems led to the development of faster, more accurate tools for calculating and record-keeping?

tax records

3. What three concepts did Jacquard's loom present that were important in computer theory?

coded on punch cards
run stored programs
automate jobs

4. What four parts in Babbage's analytical engine were similar to modern computers?

calculating
storage/retrieval
carry out inst.
reading/writing

5. What are remote terminals? Why do you think they were an important aspect of computer development?

away from mainframe.

6. What innovations suggest a fifth generation of computers?

    artificial intelligence
    voice synthesis

7. Of what significance were symbolic languages and language-translator programs?

    programmers can use English-like language to program
    in stead of machine lang

8. What was the significance of the TRS-80 and the IBM PC in the microcomputer industry?

    available in a store

9. What is involved in the hardware industry other than selling computer equipment?

Support

10. Name some problems of the early software industry.

lots of bugs.
rewrite programs for new machine
Skilled programmers were rare

CHAPTER 3

Introduction to Information Systems

❏ KEY TERMS

Application programmer The person who converts a design for a system into instructions for the computer; this person is responsible for writing, coding, testing, debugging, documenting, and implementing programs.

Audit trail A means of verifying the accuracy of information, it consists of a description of the path that leads to the original data upon which information is based.

Computer-aided design (CAD) Process of designing, drafting, and analyzing a prospective product using computer graphics on a video terminal.

Computer-aided engineering A system used to analyze engineering designs that allows engineers to interact with the computer during simulation runs as errors are identified.

Computer operator The person responsible for setting up equipment; mounting and removing tapes, disks, and diskettes; and monitoring the operation of the computer.

Data-base administrator (DBA) The person who oversees the implementation and administration of an organization's data base(s).

Data-base analyst The person responsible for the analysis, design, and implementation of the data base.

Data-entry operator The person who transcribes data into a form suitable for computer processing.

Debug To locate, isolate, and correct errors in a program.

Feedback A check within a system to see whether predetermined goals are being met; the return of information about the effectiveness of the system.

GIGO (garbage in, garbage out) A phrase illustrating the fact that the meaningfulness of computer output relies on the accuracy or relevancy of the data fed into the processor.

Input Data submitted to the computer for processing.

Keypunch operator The person who uses a keypunch machine to transfer data from source documents to computer storage.

Librarian The person responsible for classifying, cataloging, and maintaining the files and programs stored on tapes, disks and diskettes, and all other storage media in a computer library.

Maintenance programmer The person who maintains programs by making needed changes and improvements.

Management information system (MIS) manager The person responsible for planning and tying together all the information resources of a firm.

Materials requirement planning (MRP) A manufacturing system that ties together different manufacturing needs such as raw materials planning and inventory control into interacting systems. The interacting systems allow a manufacturer to plan and control operations efficiently.

Output Information that comes from the computer as a result of processing into a form that can be used by people.

Process To transform data into useful information by classifying, sorting, calculating, summarizing, and storing.

Remote-terminal operator A person involved with preparation of input data at a location some distance from the computer itself.

Synergism Situation in which the combined efforts of all parts of an information system achieve a greater effect than the sum of the individual parts.

System A group of related elements that work together toward a common goal.

System analyst The person who is responsible for system analysis, design, and implementation of computer-based information systems and who is the communication link or interface between users and technical persons.

System programmer The person responsible for creating and maintaining system software.

The U.S. has gradually evolved from an industrial society to an information society. Today most businesses and institutions rely on computers for their information needs, and the quality of information is important to meet these needs. Meaningful information is accurate, verifiable, timely, relevant, complete, and clear. GIGO, or "garbage in-garbage out," occurs when errors enter the system and result in inaccurate reports.

Information should be accurate, or error-free, but sometimes speed is more important than accuracy. Information can be verified, or checked, in one of three ways. It can be compared with accurate information, rekeyed and processed again, or traced back to the original source by means of an audit trail. Information looses its value as it ages, so it must be kept timely, or current. Information helps decision making when it is relevant, or specific to a particular need. The completeness of information refers not to the quantity of information, but rather to its content. Circumstances can determine whether or not information is complete. Clear information has no ambiguous terms and is stated in a way that leaves no doubts about its meaning.

A system is a group of related elements that work together towards a common goal. A system is made up of input, processes, and output. In theory, a system's primary goal in survival. Feedback, from internal or external sources, helps a system survive, by pinpointing strengths and weaknesses. Many systems are subsystems of larger systems, but the boundaries between systems are not always clear.

The concept of system theory can be applied to organizations, because organizations have groups of related elements working toward common goals. Decision makers in organizations use information to increase knowledge and reduce uncertainty. Information is data that has been processed and made useful for decision making. Thus, organizations have information systems to transform data into information and make it available to decision makers in a timely fashion.

An information system consists of hardware, software, data, and people. Hardware is the equipment or parts of the computer that can be seen. Input equipment puts data in the computer. Processing equipment manipulates data. Output equipment transfers processed data from one location to another. Software consists of instructions needed to run computers. System programs run the computer itself and application programs solve a user's problems. Data is collected, changed to a form the computer can use, and processed into information. People coordinate all activities within the system. Providers design and operate the computer information system. Users interact directly with the information system, and clients benefit from the system although they may not interact directly with the system.

Synergism is a relationship in which the efforts of all of the parts are greater than the sum of the efforts of each part independently. The combination of hardware, software, data, and people creates synergistic relationships.

The degree to which information reduces uncertainty determines its value to the organization. An organization quantifies that value by the comparing the cost of obtaining information with the cost of making a decision without the information. The information loses value if the cost of the former exceeds the cost of the latter.

Businesses use computer-based information systems in a variety of ways. The primary uses were clerical and record keeping tasks. Today, computers are also used for operational functions and strategic planning. The accounting profession was one of the first to use computers, and payroll is a common application. An information system designed for budgeting can process data and generate reports that are used to manage financial resources. Order processing can provide fast and accurate movement of customer orders. A computerized inventory system can help process orders, and helps reduce costs and prevent order delays.

Human resources management provides employee services such as training, relocation and benefits, policies and procedures, and personnel record keeping. Personnel record keeping is ideally suited to computerization because a large volume of data must be updated frequently.

Materials requirement planning (MRP) aids in the planning, purchasing, and control of raw materials used in the manufacture of goods. MRP subsystems control inventory, schedule facilities, design and test new products, and hold down costs.

Computer-aided engineering systems are used in the design of products. They are used for everything from initial idea to production drawings. An engineer can identify and correct mistakes during a simulation run.

People wanting careers in computer fields have a wide choice of work including jobs in data-processing operations, which includes librarians, computer operators, and data-entry jobs.

System development personnel include programmers and system analysts. Application programmers create programs for specific user functions such as accounting and word processing. System programmers develop programs that operate the computer. Maintenance programmers work on keeping existing programs up to date and debugged, or error free. System analysts work on the analysis, design, and implementation of formal systems.

Data-base specialists design and control the use of data resources. A data-base analyst plans and coordinates data use within a system. The data-base administrator (DBA) controls all of the data resources in an organization.

A management information system (MIS) manager is responsible for planning and tying together all the information resources of a firm, including physical and human resources, and must devise effective controls to monitor progress toward company goals.

Professional associations assist computer professionals by keeping abreast of developments, certifying computer professionals, coordinating different societies, educating students, and encouraging high standards. Some are AFIPS (American Federation of Information Processing Societies), ACM (Association for Computing Machinery), DPMA (Data Processing Management Association), ASM (Association of Systems Management), ICCP (Institute of Certification of Computer Professionals), and SIM (Society for Information Management).

❑ STRUCTURED LEARNING

1. The qualities of information include _____.
   a. timeliness, completeness, effectiveness
   b. clarity, longevity, accuracy
   c. relevancy, verifiability, synergism
   d. accuracy, timeliness, clarity

---

d. Effectiveness and synergistic might describe a system after it gets high-quality information. Longevity occurs if the system is able to change.

2. The U.S. has evolved from a(n) _____ to a(n) _____ society in the twentieth century.
   a. industrial, information
   b. information, industrial
   c. agricultural, industrial
   d. industrial, agricultural

---

a. As the need for information increased, technology was developed to meet that need and gradually information related jobs outnumbered industrial jobs.

3. A system is affected by _____.
   a. external factors and internal factors
   b. system theory
   c. input, processing, and output
   d. boundaries

---

a. The system is affected by external factors beyond its control such as the economy and laws, and internal factors such as the quality of its management, employees, communication channels, and departmental relationships.

4. To trace information back to its source, conduct a(n) _____.
   a. information trail
   b. audit trail
   c. data trac
   d. data trail

---

b. An audit trail describes the path that leads to the data upon which information is based.

5. The boundaries between systems _____.
    a. must be clear and rigid   c. are not always easy to define
    b. should be non-existent   d. should be seen as a whole concept

---

c. Each system can be viewed in terms of inputs, processes, outputs, and feedback mechanisms. The boundaries and elements of a system depend on the level or scope at which one views the system.

6. The four major components of an information system are _____.
    a. hardware, peripherals, people, data   c. hardware, software, data, people
    b. hardware, software, data, peripherals   d. software, data, people, peripherals

---

c. Peripherals are printers, disk drives, and so on, and they are part of the hardware.

7. The value of information is retained if _____.
    a. it survives the effects of external factors
    b. the cost of getting the information exceeds the ill effects of making decisions without the information
    c. the information retains synergism
    d. the cost of getting the information is less than the potential cost of making the decision without the information

---

d. The degree to which information reduces uncertainty will be too costly if a decision could have been made at less cost without the information.

8. The person who helps the user determine information needs and designs a new system is the _____.
    a. application programmer   c. chief executive officer
    b. MIS manager   d. system analyst

---

d. The system analyst is also trained to gather information about existing systems, analyze the existing system, and recommend changes to the existing systems.

9. When computers were first used in businesses, little emphasis was put on _____.
    a. processing speed
    b. cost containment
    c. centralized planning
    d. long-term storage devices

---

c. At first, computers were used mainly to solve specific processing problems and little planning went into how the machines could benefit the entire organization.

10. Personnel/record keeping is ideally suited to computerization because _____.
    a. the data is easy to enter and process
    b. it does not require extensive calculations
    c. it uses small amounts of computer memory
    d. the volume of information is large and needs frequent updating

---

d. Most organizations keep employee records in a centralized data base to which additions, deletions, and other changes are made.

❏ TRUE/FALSE

1. T F Limitations in time and money may necessitate compromises in the quality of information.

2. T F Good information is timeless and never loses its value.

3. T F One way of verifying the accuracy of information is rekeying the data and comparing it with the original.

4. T F In system theory, a system's primary goal is speed.

5. T F Despite some innovations, the only efficient and accurate input method is keyboarding.

6. T F An adequate analysis of a company's information needs need consider only internal factors.

7. T F In an information system, clients interact directly with the system.

8. T F In an information system, workers such as programmers, system analysts, and operators are grouped in a category called providers.

9. T F A synergistic system is one in which data is processed into information.

10. T F One goal of inventory control systems is to ensure that there is not an overload of items that tie up operating capital.

❑ MATCHING

a. application programmers
b. DBA
c. MRP
d. audit trail
e. feedback

f. system
g. CAE
h. synergism
i. remote terminal operator
j. librarian

j 1. The person responsible for classifying, cataloging, and maintaining files and programs stored on disks and tapes is the _____.

d 2. Tracing information back to its original sources is a(n) _____.

f 3. A group of related elements working together towards a common goal is a(n) _____.

g 4. A type of system used to design and test products is _____.

b 5. The person who controls all the data resources of an organization is the _____.

e 6. _____ helps a system survive by pinpointing the system's strengths and weaknesses.

i 7. The person who is involved in data input is the _____.

a 8. People who write programs designed to solve a particular user need are _____.

h 9. When the combined efforts of the parts is greater than the sum of the efforts of each part operating independently, the relation is a(n) _____.

c 10. A system that assists in the planning, purchasing, and control of raw materials used in manufacturing is _____.

❑ SHORT ANSWER

1. What must information be, to be meaningful?

   timely
   relevant
   accurate
   verifable
   complete
   clear

2. When is information considered timely?

When its Current

3. Name the three ways of verifying information.

compare
review
audit

4. What is the primary goal of a system?

Survival

5. What is information? What are the components of an information system?

process data

hardware
software
data
people

6. What is one primary goal of most of the associations to which computer professionals can belong?

high standards & up to date

7. Describe the work of a maintenance programmer. What special abilities are helpful?

revise, maintain, debug

programming
analytical

8. How are people part of an information system?

providers
users
clients

9. A well-designed MRP system has many interacting subsystems. Describe the effects of three interactive subsystems in an MRP system.

inventory control

10. How is a computer inventory system facilitate order processing?

CHAPTER 4

Hardware

Address A unique identifier assigned to each memory location.

American Standard Code for Information Interchange (ASCII) A seven-bit standard code used for information interchange among data-processing systems, communication systems, and associated equipment.

Arithmetic/logic unit (ALU) The section of the processor or CPU that handles arithmetic computations and logical operations.

ASCII-8 An eight-bit version of ASCII developed for computers that require eight-bit, rather than seven-bit, codes.

Binary (base 2) number system Number system for computer operations that uses the digits 0 and 1 and has a base of 2; corresponds to the two states in machine circuitry, on and off.

Binary representation Use of a two-state, or binary, system to represent data.

Binary system A two-state system used to represent data. The states are "on" or "off."

Bit cells The name for memory locations in semiconductors.

Bubble memory A memory medium in which data is represented by magnetized spots (magnetic domains) resting on a thin film of semiconductor material.

Cache memory Also known as a high-speed buffer; a working buffer or temporary area used to help speed the execution of a program.

Central processing unit (CPU) Acts as the "brain" of the computer; composed of three sections_arithmetic/logic unit (ALU), control unit, and memory unit.

Check bit Another name for parity bit.

Clock speed The number of electronic pulses a microprocessor can produce per second.

Control unit The section of the CPU that directs the sequence of operations by electrical signals and governs the actions of the various units that make up the computer.

Decimal number system A number system based on the powers of 10.

Dump A paper copy of the contents of computer memory; valuable for debugging programs.

Erasable programmable read-only memory (EPROM) A form of read-only memory that can be erased and reprogrammed, but only by being submitted to a special process such as exposure to ultraviolet light.

Even parity A method of coding in which an even number of 1 bits represent each character; used to increase the detection of errors.

Extended Binary Coded Decimal Interchange Code (EBCDIC) An eight-bit code for character representation.

Four-bit binary coded decimal (BCD) A four-bit computer code that uses four-bit groupings to represent digits in decimal numbers.

Hard-wired instructions Instructions programmed into memory circuitry by the manufacturer that cannot be changed or deleted by other stored-program instructions.

Hexadecimal (base 16) number system A base 16 number system commonly used when printing the contents of memory to aid programmers in finding errors.

K (kilobyte) A symbol used to represent 1,024 (2^{10}) memory units (1,024 bytes) when referring to a computer's memory capacity; often rounded to 1,000 bytes.

Magnetic domain A magnetized spot representing data in bubble memory.

Megahertz (MHz) One million times per second; the unit of measurement for the speed of a computer's clock.

Memory The section of the CPU that holds instructions, data, and intermediate and final results during processing; also called primary memory, internal memory, and main memory.

Microprogram A sequence of instructions wired into read-only memory (ROM); used to tailor a system to meet the user's specific processing requirements.

Next-sequential-instruction feature The ability of a computer to execute program steps in the order in which they are stored in memory unless branching takes place.

Nondestructive read/destructive write Feature of computer memory that permits data to be read and retained in its original state, so that it can be repeatedly referenced during processing.

Numeric bits The four rightmost bit positions of 6-bit BCD used to encode numeric data.

Octal (base 8) number system Number system in which each position represents a power of eight.

Odd parity A method of coding in which an odd number of 1 bits is used to represent each character; facilitates error checking.

Operand The part of an instruction that tells the computer where to find the data or equipment on which to operate.

Operation code (op code) The part of an instruction that tells what operation is to be done.

Parity bit A bit added to detect incorrect transmission of data; it conducts internal checks to determine whether the correct number of 0 or 1 bits is present.

Processor The term used to refer collectively to the ALU and control unit.

Programmable read-only memory (PROM) Read-only memory that can be programmed by the manufacturer or by the user for special functions to meet the unique needs of the user.

Random-access memory (RAM) Form of memory into which instructions and data can be read, written and erased; directly accessed by the computer; volatile.

Read-only memory (ROM) Computer hardware that contains instructions that cannot be deleted or changed by stored-program instructions because they are wired into the computer.

Reading The process of accessing the same instructions or data over and over.

Register An internal computer component used for temporary storage of an instruction or data; capable of accepting, holding, and transferring that instruction or data very rapidly.

Semiconductor memory Memory composed of circuitry on silicon chips; smaller and more expensive than core memory; allows for faster processing and requires a constant power source.

Silicon chip Solid-logic circuitry on a small piece of silicon used to form the memory of third- and fourth-generation computers.

Six-bit binary coded decimal (BCD) A data representation scheme that is used to represent the decimal digits 0 through 9, the letters A through Z, and 28 special characters.

Storage Also referred to as secondary, external, or auxiliary storage; supplements memory and is external to the CPU; data is accessed at slower speeds.

Stored program Instructions held in the computer's memory in electronic form; can be executed repeatedly at the computer's own speed.

Stored-program concept The idea that program instructions can be stored in memory in electrical form so that no human intervention is required during processing; allows the computer to process the instructions at its own speed.

Variable A meaningful name assigned by the programmer that stands for a value.

Word A storage location within memory.

Word size The number of bits that can be manipulated at one time.

Writing The process of storing new instructions or data in computer memory.

Zone bit A bit used in different combinations with numeric bits to represent numbers, letters, and special characters.

❑ SUMMARY

The heart of the computer system, the central processing unit (CPU), has three parts: the control unit, the arithmetic/logic unit (ALU), and memory. The control unit and the ALU are referred to as the processor, which may be on one or more circuit elements or "chips".

Data and programs in the CPU are held in memory, which is volatile, or non-permanent; thus, data is lost when the electricity is turned off or disrupted unless it has been saved on storage such as disks or tapes. Memory (also called primary memory, internal memory, or main memory) holds instructions, data, and intermediate and final results of processing.

The control unit controls activity in the CPU and directs the sequence of instructions. Data is manipulated in the ALU. The computations include addition, subtraction, multiplication, and division. Logical comparisons include six combinations of equality: equal to, not equal to, greater than, less than, equal to or greater than, and equal to or less than.

A computer processes instructions. Each instruction has two parts: operation code (op code), which tells the control unit what function to perform, and the operand, which indicates the location of data to operate upon. Computers perform instructions sequentially. This next-sequential-instruction feature requires that instructions be placed in consecutive locations in memory. Computers can only execute one instruction at a time.

The development of the stored-program concept increased processing speed by storing instructions and data in memory. Once instructions are stored, they remain in memory until new ones are stored over them. Executing the same instructions over and over is known as reading. Storing new instructions is called writing. Together these actions are known as nondestructive read/destructive write. Instructions placed in memory are called stored programs. A location in memory is an address. A variable is a symbolic name for data to be changed; it represents a location to the programmer. The computer locates data by the address location.

Memory is usually semiconductor memory composed of circuitry on silicon chips. The data is stored on these chips in locations called bit cells, which are arranged in matrices. Another form of memory is bubble memory, which consists of magnetized spots, or magnetic domains, resting on a thin film of semiconductor memory.

Random-access memory (RAM) is used to store programs and data during processing. It is known as the working area of the computer, where nondestructive read/destructive write occurs. This type of memory requires a constant source of power, or the data is lost.

Read-only memory (ROM)—sometimes called firmware—holds instructions that are hard wired and cannot be changed or deleted by other stored-program instructions. Microprograms are sequences of instructions for jobs such as calculating square roots that would otherwise have to be directed at much slower speeds by instructions stored in RAM. Programmable read-only memory (PROM) can be programmed once by the user. A mistake in the program is permanent. Erasable programmable read-only memory (EPROM) can be erased by an ultraviolet process.

A register is a temporary holding area in the CPU, but not part of memory. Cache memory, a high speed buffer, helps speed processing by serving as a working buffer or temporary holding area to store data and instructions. It can be either part of main memory or an independent high-speed storage device.

Storage (auxiliary or external) is outside of the CPU and data is transferred between memory and storage through electrical lines. Memory in early computers consisted of units of magnetic core. Each could store one bit (binary digit) and was magnetized. Today semiconductor memory is made of circuits on silicon chips. Data is stored in bit cells. Another form of storage, bubble memory, consists of magnetized spots (magnetic domains) resting on semiconductor material.

Microprocessors are categorized by their speed and the amount of memory they can access. The speed depends on two factors: word size and clock speed. The word size is the number of bits that the microprocessor can process at one time. The clock speed, measured in megahertz (MHz), represents the number of electronic pulses the chip can produce each second.

Data is represented in the computer by the electrical state of the machine's circuitry, either "on" or "off." This two-state system is known as a binary system, and its use to represent data is called binary representation. This is the binary (base 2) number system and operates similarly to the decimal number system.

Storage locations within memory are called words. Word sizes are measured in lengths of 8, 16, 24, 32, 48, and 64 bits. The octal (base 8) number system, 0 through 7, is a short method of representing data in one word. Three binary digits equal one octal.

When a program fails to execute correctly, it helps to examine the contents of the memory locations, which are output on a printout called a dump. A dump is usually printed in the hexadecimal (base 16) number system, 0 through 15 and A through F.

Binary notation becomes complex when dealing with large numbers, so other coding schemes are used instead. The four-bit binary coded decimal (BCD) represents each decimal digit in a number using four bits. This saves space, is easier to convert to its decimal equivalent, and allows 16 bit combinations. Six-bit BCD allows 64 combinations. The four right bits are called numeric bits and the two left bits are zone bits. Extended Binary Coded Decimal Interchange Code (EBCDIC), an eight-bit code, allows 256 bit combinations. American Standard Code for Information Interchange (ASCII) is a seven-bit code similar to ASCII-8. Bits used together are a byte. One K (kilobyte) equals 1024 units.

A parity bit or check bit is used to detect errors. An odd number of 1 bits for a character is odd parity. An even number of 1 bits is even parity.

❑ STRUCTURED LEARNING

1. A processor built on several circuit boards in a boxlike structure is _____.
   a. an ALU
   b. a mainframe
   c. a control unit
   d. a high-speed buffer

b. A processor may incorporate one or more circuit elements or "chips" built in frames, thus, the name mainframe.

2. In what part of the CPU is data manipulated?
   a. primary unit
   b. memory unit
   c. control unit
   d. arithmetic/logic unit

d. The ALU performs arithmetic computations including addition, subtraction, multiplication, and division.

3. To what does the characteristic nondestructive read/destructive write apply?
   a. stored-program concept
   b. ALU
   c. variables
   d. word size

---

a. Nondestructive read/destructive write refers to the way memory is used; thus, it is characteristic of stored programs.

4. Microprograms are _____.
   a. programs used in microcomputers
   b. programs that use random access memory
   c. programs that the user tailors to his own needs
   d. a direct result of hard-wiring

---

d. Microprograms are sequences of instructions built into read-only memory. They are supplied by computer manufacturers and cannot be changed.

5. Clock speed represents _____.
   a. the number of bits that can be processed by the microcomputer at one time
   b. the speed of memory
   c. the speed of bit cells
   d. the number of electronic pulses a chip can produce each second

---

d. Clock speed describes a microprocessor. It is built in and is measured in megahertz.

6. RAM memory is volatile; this means _____.
   a. its contents will be lost if the power is disrupted
   b. it will burn if placed near fire
   c. it cannot be erased or rewritten
   d. it performs at a very high speed

---

a. RAM memory is not permanent and data is erased when the computer is turned off. Data must be saved on external storage.

7. The two parts of a computer instruction are the _____.
   a. control unit and the logic unit
   b. operation code and the operand
   c. variable and address
   d. operand and the data

---

b. The operation code indicates to the control unit what function is to be performed. The operand indicates the memory location of the data.

8. A variable is _____.
   a. the term for the changing on/off states of electric current
   b. another name for random-access memory
   c. a name for a kind of a data to be changed
   d. a term for the various bit code sizes

---

c. Sometimes data must be changed, added, or deleted during program execution. The variable is the name of the location where the data to be changed is located. The variable name does not change, only the data stored in that location.

9. Most computers detect the occurrence of an error by means of a _____.
   a. parity bit
   b. six-bit BCD
   c. dump
   d. high-speed buffer

---

a. An additional bit called a parity bit is put in each memory location to adjust the number of 1 bits or 0 bits to even or odd, depending on whether parity is even or odd. The circuitry monitors its operation by checking to be sure that the required number of 1 bits or 0 bits is present at each location.

10. A major reason Extended Binary Coded Decimal Interchange Code was developed is that it _____.
   a. can be sent over telephone lines
   b. is written in everyday English
   c. allows 256 bit combinations
   d. represents only uppercase letters

---

c. EBCDIC is an 8-bit code giving 2^8 possibilities. It can be used to represent uppercase, lowercase letters, and special characters such as percent and quotation mark.

❏ TRUE/FALSE

1. T F   Computers can easily execute many instructions simultaneously.   F

2. T F   Arithmetic computations occur in memory.   F

3. T F   A variable is so named because the name of the memory address changes or varies as   F
          needed by the user.

4. T F   The process of accessing the same instructions or data over and over is called reading.

5. T F   Semiconductors store data in locations called matrices.   F

6. T F   When data is lost through a power failure, it is called a "dump" by programmers.   F

7. T F   Odd parity is when a bit is lost through transfer of data from one device to another.   F

8. T F   The next-sequential-instruction concept refers to how a computer performs instructions.

9. T F   The most common storage media are domains and bit cells.   F

10. T F   Read-only memory (ROM) instructions are hard-wired and cannot be changed or   deleted
          by stored-program instructions.

❏ MATCHING

a. parity
b. PROM
c. control unit
d. address
e. variable

f. cache memory
g. EPROM
h. words
i. dump
j. microprocessor

1. The part of the CPU that maintains order and controls activity, but does not process or store data is
the ___c___.

2. A portion of memory used to speed the processing operations is called a high-speed buffer, or ___f___.

3. Memory locations are referred to as ___h___.

4. Computers guard against errors through the use of a check bit known as a(n) ___a___ bit.

5. The contents of memory locations can be represented in hexadecimal form in a list called a(n) ___i___.

6. A symbolic name the programmer assigns to the data stored in memory is a(n) ___e___.

7. In order to find data, each location in memory is assigned a(n) _____.

8. Word size and clock speed describe a(n) _____.

9. A version of read-only memory that can be programmed by the user is _____.

10. Read-only memory that can be erased by a special process such as ultraviolet light is called _____.

❑ SHORT ANSWER

1. Name the three parts of the central processing unit.

    ALU
    Control
    memory

2. Logical comparisons include six combinations of equality. Name them.

    =
    ≠
    >
    <
    ≥
    ≤

3. What is semiconductor memory?

circuitry on silicon chips.
chips store data in bit cells (on/off) arranged in matrices.

4. How is read-only memory different from nondestructive read?

ROM cannot be overwritten
RAM while read-only can be overwritten

5. What are the 16 characters used in the hexadecimal (base 16) number system? How do they facilitate making sense of a dump?

0-9
A-f

6. Convert this binary number to a decimal number. Show your work.

1 1 0 0 1 0 0 1

7 6 5 4 3 2 1 0

128+64 + 8 + 1 = 301

7. Convert this octal number to a decimal number. Show your work.

2 3 0 5

8. Name three coding schemes other than binary notation.

hexidecimal   ASCII

decimal   EBCDIC

octal.   ASCII-8

9. Name and describe the two parts of the instruction code.

Operation code - what to do
operand - where address location

10. How do semiconductors store data in bit cells?

bit cells arranged in matrices   8 rows by 8 columns

CHAPTER 5

Input and Output

❏ KEY TERMS

Amount field The field where a clerk manually inserts the amount of the check; used in the processing of bank checks.

Bar-code reader A device used to read a bar code by means of reflected light, such as a scanner that reads the Universal Product Code on supermarket products.

Chain printer An output device that has the character set engraved in type and assembled in a chain that revolves horizontally past all print positions; prints when a print hammer (one for each column of the paper) presses the paper against an inked ribbon that presses against the characters on the print chain.

Composite monitor A monitor with composite color and resolution slightly better than a TV.

Continuous form Forms or paper in a single ribbon, such as cash register tape.

Cut form Forms or paper cut up into single units, such as a phone or utility bill.

Daisy-wheel printer An output device resembling an office typewriter; it has a flat disk with petal-like projections with characters on the surfaces; printing occurs one character at a time.

Dot-matrix printer (wire-matrix printer) A type of impact printer that creates characters formed by the activation of dots in a matrix.

Drum printer An impact printer that consists of a metal cylinder with rows of characters engraved on its surface; one line of print is produced with each rotation of the drum.

Electrostatic printer A nonimpact printer in which electromagnetic impulses and heat are used to affix characters to paper.

Electrothermal printer A nonimpact printer that uses special heat-sensitive paper; characters are formed when heated rods in a matrix touch the paper.

Flat panel display An output screen most commonly used on portable computers; three common types are liquid-crystal, gas plasma, and electroluminescent.

Graphic display device   A visual display device that projects output in the form of graphs and line drawings and accepts input from a keyboard or light pen.

Graphics tablet   A flat, board-like object that, when drawn on, transfers the image to a computer screen.

Impact printer   A printer that forms characters by physically striking a ribbon against paper.

Ink-jet printer   A nonimpact printer that uses streams of charged ink to form dot-matrix characters.

I/O   Short for input/output.

Laser printer   A type of nonimpact printer that combines laser beams and electrophotographic technology to form images on paper.

Light pen   A pen-shaped object with a photoelectric cell at its end used to draw lines on a visual display screen.

Magnetic disk   A direct-access storage medium that is a metal platter coated on both sides with a magnetized recording material upon which data are stored as magnetized spots.

Magnetic-ink character reader   A device used to scan magnetic-ink characters.

Magnetic-ink character recognition (MICR)   A process that involves reading characters composed of magnetized particles; often used to sort checks for subsequent processing.

Magnetic tape   A sequential storage medium that is a narrow strip of plastic upon which spots of iron oxide are magnetized to represent data.

Monochrome monitor   A computer monitor that displays amber, green, or white characters on a black background.

Mouse   A hardware input device used to move the pointers or cursors on systems with graphical user interfaces such as the Macintosh; movement of the pointer on the display screen corresponds to the movement of the mouse on the desk or tabletop.

Nonimpact printer   A device that uses heat, laser technology, or photographic techniques to print output.

On-us field   The section of a check that contains the customer's checking account number.

Optical character   A special type of character that can be read by an optical-character reader.

Optical-character recognition (OCR) A method of electronic scanning that reads numbers, letters, and other characters and then converts the optical images into appropriate electrical signals.

Optical-mark page reader A device that senses marks on an OMR document as the document passes under a light source.

Optical-mark recognition (OMR) Mark sensing; a method of electronic scanning that reads marks on a page and converts the optical images into appropriate electrical signals.

Plotter An output device that prepares graphic, hard copy information by using pens; it can produce lines, curves, and complex shapes.

Point-of-sale (POS) system A computerized system that records information required for such things as inventory control and accounting at the point where a product is sold.

Point-of-sale (POS) terminal An input device that records information at the point where a product is sold.

Print-wheel printer An impact printer with 120 print wheels, each containing 48 characters. To produce characters on paper, the print wheels rotate into position, forming an entire line of characters, then a hammer presses paper against the wheels.

Remote terminal A terminal that is placed at a location distant from the central computer.

RGB (red-green-blue) monitor A computer monitor that displays in three colors with high-resolution.

Scanner A device that reads printed material so that it can be put in a computer-readable form without having to retype, redraw, reprint, or rephotograph the material.

Source-data automation The use of special equipment to collect data at its point of origin.

Touch-tone device A type of terminal used with ordinary telephone lines to transmit data.

Transit field The section of a check, preprinted with magnetic ink, that includes the bank identification number.

Universal Product Code (UPC) A machine-readable code consisting of thirty vertical dark bars and twenty-nine spaces that identifies a product and its manufacturer; commonly used on most grocery items.

Visual display terminal A terminal capable of receiving output on a cathode-ray tube (CRT) and, with special provisions, is capable of transmitting data through a keyboard.

Voice recognition A method of data entry that involves speaking into a microphone attached to a computer system.

Voice synthesizer A method of computer output that provides information to users in the form of sequences of sound that resemble the human voice.

Wand reader A device used in reading source data represented in bar-code or character form.

Xerographic printer A type of nonimpact printer that uses printing methods similar to those used in common xerographic copying machines.

❑ SUMMARY

Input is data submitted to the computer for processing. Output is the information produced by the computer as a result of processing. These processes are often referred to as I/O. Until recently, most data was entered into a computer by punched cards. Today, however, more efficient methods of data entry are used. Key-to-magnetic media data entry, or keyboarding, is the most widely used method of input today. Data items are stored as magnetized spots on tape or disk surfaces. Other input devices enable the user to control the cursor (or symbol on the screen that shows where the next character will be entered) without using the keyboard. These devices are mice, graphics tablets, light pens, scanners, and microphones (used in voice recognition systems).

Source-data automation speeds the speed, accuracy, and efficiency of gathering data by collecting data about an event, in computer-readable form, when and where data is generated. Several approaches are available. Magnetic-ink character recognition (MICR) uses a magnetic-ink character reader to detect iron oxide in the ink. The presence of a magnetic field is a 1 bit. MICR is used for check processing in the banking industry. Optical-mark recognition (OMR) or mark-sensing, uses an optical-mark page reader to detect light reflected from a mark on paper. One version of OMR, the bar-code reader, recognizes patterns of lines known as bar-codes. These are used in point-of-sale (POS) systems. The most familiar is the Universal Product Code (UPC). The UPC can be read by a hand-held wand or a fixed scanner. Optical-character recognition (OCR) devices recognize shapes of marks as characters rather than the positions. Remote terminals, also called point-of-sale terminals, collect data at the source and send it to a central computer. Touch-tone devices are remote terminals using telephones to send data.

Data is output through printers, plotters, and visual display terminals (VDTs). Printers are output devices that print processed data in a form that humans can read. This permanent record is termed hard copy. The two types of printers are impact and nonimpact.

Impact printers print one character or one line at a time by pressing print elements together with inked ribbon and paper. Two character-at-a-time devices are the dot-matrix (or wire-matrix) printer, which uses a matrix composed of pins in various combinations to form characters, and the daisy-wheel printer, which uses a flat disk with rotating petal-like projections each containing a character. Line-at-a-time printers include print wheel, chain, and drum printers.

Nonimpact printers do not use striking mechanisms to imprint characters. An electrostatic printer uses charged ink particles that are attracted to paper of an opposite charge. Electrothermal printers use heated rods near heat sensitive paper. An ink-jet printer sprays charged ink onto the paper. Laser printers focus light beams through a rotating disk onto paper. Xerographic printers are similar to photocopy machines. Nonimpact printers are generally faster and more reliable than impact because they have fewer parts.

Plotters are output devices that print graphics with pens. They often produce line and bar charts.

VDTs are output devices that display data on cathode-ray tubes (CRT) similar to TV screens. They produce soft copy (temporary or nonpermanent output) and are much faster than printers. A graphic display device is a CRT that can display drawings, graphs, charts, and complex curves and shapes. Graphics monitors are used in computer-assisted design/computer-assisted manufacturing (CAD/CAM). VDTs are often called monitors. There are three types: monochrome, composite color, and RGB. There are also flat panel displays used on portable microcomputers. Soft copy is also produced by voice synthesizers, which output data in sequences of sound that resemble the human voice.

❑ STRUCTURED LEARNING

1. Mice, light pens, and graphics tablets are _____.
    a. forms of cursors
    b. methods of source-data automation
    c. input devices
    d. types of keyboards

c. They are input devices that enable the user to bypass the keyboard, yet they require a human to input the data and thus are not forms of source-data automation.

2. The information produced by a computer as a result of processing is referred to as _____.
    a. data
    b. input
    c. output
    d. files

c. Data consists of raw unprocessed facts that are input to a computer system. A file is a collection of records.

3. The main advantage of source-data automation is that it _____.
    a. is a method of bypassing the keyboard
    b. uses OCR
    c. improves speed, accuracy, and efficiency of data-processing operations
    d. can be implemented in several ways

c. By eliminating the rekeying of data and providing a direct method of input, source-data automation improves data collection.

4. A major application of magnetic-ink character recognition is _____.
   a. grocery check-out registers
   b. scoring examination sheets
   c. processing bank checks
   d. transferring data over telephone lines

c. The magnetic-ink characters are printed along the bottom of the check. The checks are sorted by bank number and routed back to the customer.

5. Collecting data in computer-readable form when and where the event takes place is called _____.
   a. source-data automation
   b. I/O operations
   c. keyboarding
   d. OMR

a. There are several methods of source-data automation and all methods reduce errors in data entry and improve speed and efficiency.

6. The fastest printers are usually _____ printers.
   a. impact
   b. dot-matrix
   c. nonimpact
   d. plotters

c. Nonimpact printers involve less physical movement than impact printers because they have fewer movable mechanical parts.

7. The inability of nonimpact printers to make carbons is overcome by _____.
   a. speed
   b. letter quality print
   c. the use of plain paper
   d. the ability to print directly through one paper onto another

a. Nonimpact printers can produce several copies in less time than impact printers can produce one page with several carbons.

8. POS systems are used for _____.
    a. magnetic-ink character recognition   c. source-data automation
    b. binary notation   d. error checking

---

c. POS systems have scanners that read tags or UPC labels. The data is then sent to the computer.

9. Printers that produce hard copy by activating print elements that are pressed against paper are called printers.
    a. ink jet   c. electrostatic
    b. xerographic   d. impact

---

d. Ink jet, xerographic, and electrostatic are all examples of nonimpact printers.

10. The output device best used for applications involving inquiry and response is the _____.
    a. voice synthesizer   c. laser printer
    b. VDT   d. keyboard

---

b. The VDT enables the user to see immediately what is being typed (the question) and displays the requested information much faster than a printer would. The information requested might be entirely too voluminous to merit using a voice synthesizer. In addition, the user can edit or extract portions of the information.

❏ TRUE/FALSE

1. T F   It is not possible to produce a hard-copy output with a visual display terminal.

2. T F   Laser printers function very much like a xerographic copy machine.

3. T F   A chain printer can print a variety of characters including italics and boldface simply by changing fonts.

4. T F   Cut forms, such as phone or utility bills can be read and sorted by an OCR device.

5. T F   Optical mark recognition (OMR) is sometimes called mark sensing.

6. T F   The majority of data entry is done manually by human data-entry personnel.

7. T F   Scanners have become more popular with the increased interest in desktop publishing.

8. T F Source-data automation involves collecting data in machine-readable form, when and where the data originates.

9. T F The UPC codes the price of an item. _F_

10. T F The I/O operations of any computer-based system are the communication links between people and the machines.

❏ MATCHING

a. flat-panel display	f. UPC
b. RGB monitor	g. dot-matrix printer
c. continuous form	h. plotter
d. hard copy	i. OMR
e. print-wheel printer	j. wand reader

_f_ 1. Probably the most widely known bar-code is the _____.

_c_ 2. Data can be fed into an OCR device from a(n) _____ such as a cash register tape.

_h_ 3. An output device that prepares graphic, hard-copy information is called a(n) _____.

_e_ 4. An example of a line-at-a-time printer is the _____.

_i_ 5. One method of reading a document by passing it under a light source and recording the reflected light is _____.

_b_ 6. A monitor that receives three different color signals is a(n) _____.

_j_ 7. A UPC symbol can be read by a(n) _____ or a fixed scanner.

_d_ 8. A permanent readable copy of computer output is called a(n) _____.

_g_ 9. An impact printer in which the print element consists of a seven by five rectangular arrangement of pins is a(n) _____.

_a_ 10. A type of monitor that may be LCD or electroluminescent is the _____.

1. What is the major difference between optical-character recognition and optical-mark recognition?

detects shapes   *bars only.*

2. List some disadvantages of nonimpact printers.

No carbons

3. What is key-to-magnetic media data entry?

Keyed at Keyboard & stored on tape or disk.

4. Why has data entry traditionally been the weakest link in the chain of data processing operations?

Keying errors

5. How does the Universal Product Code facilitate source-data automation?

Code read by scanner + uses computer data instead of person keying data

6. Explain the major difference between impact and nonimpact printers.

*Impact strikes page
non-impact uses heat/laser*

7. Describe a dot-matrix printer.

uses pins that strike paper

8. Name some types of nonimpact printers.

injet
laser
electrostatic

9. What are some advantages of visual display terminals over printers?

- see output instantly
- No need to print

10. What individual components make up a POS terminal?

Keyboard
display panel
Printer for receipts

CHAPTER 6

Storage Devices

❑ KEY TERMS

Access mechanism   The device that positions the read/write head of a direct-access device over a particular track.

Backup copy   A second copy of an original tape or disk made to prevent data loss.

Blocks (blocked records)   Records grouped on magnetic tape or magnetic disk to reduce the number of interrecord gaps and more fully utilize the storage medium.

Charge-coupled device (CCD)   A storage device made of silicon that is nearly 100 times faster than bubble memory devices.

Compact disk (CD)   A nonerasable 4 3/4-inch disk used as a storage medium for microcomputers; it can store about 1,000 times more bytes than a single-sided floppy disk.

Cylinder   The tracks on all disk surfaces that may be read without repositioning the read/write arm.

Disk address   The method used to uniquely identify a data record on a magnetic disk; consists of the disk surface number, the track number, and the record number.

Disk drive   The mechanical device used to rotate a disk pack during data transmission.

Disk pack   A stack of magnetic disks.

Floppy disk (flexible disk, diskette)   A low-cost, direct-access form of data storage made of plastic and coated with a magnetizable substance upon which data are stored; disks generally come in 3 1/2- and 5 1/4-inch diameter sizes.

Interblock gap (IBG)   A space on magnetic tape that facilitates processing; separates records grouped together as blocks on the tape.

Interrecord gap (IRG)   A space that separates records stored on magnetic tape; allows the tape drive to regain speed during processing.

Laser storage system A storage device using laser technology to encode data onto a metallic surface; usually used for mass storage.

Magnetic disk A direct-access storage medium that is a metal platter coated on both sides with a magnetic recording material upon which data are stored in the form of magnetized spots.

Magnetic tape A sequential storage medium that is a narrow strip of plastic upon which spots of iron oxide are magnetized to represent data.

Optical disk A storage medium that stores data as the presence or absence of a pit burned into the surface of the disk by a laser beam.

Random-access memory (RAM) disk A portion of RAM memory that is temporarily treated as a storage device.

Read/write head An electromagnet used as a component of a tape or disk drive; in reading data, it detects magnetized areas and translates them into electrical pulses; in writing data, it magnetizes appropriate areas and erases data stored previously.

Read/write notch The oblong or rectangular opening in the jacket of a floppy disk through which the read/write head accesses the disk.

Tape drive A device that moves magnetic tape past a read/write head.

Track A horizontal row along the length of a magnetic tape on which data can be recorded; one of a series of concentric circles on the surface of a magnetic disk.

Superconductor A metal that is capable of transmitting high levels of current.

❏ SUMMARY

Memory and storage are the two types of data holding areas in a computer system. Memory is used in the CPU to store data and instructions needed for processing. Memory cannot hold all of the data used in processing, so storage holds data in amounts too large to fit in memory. Storage devices are connected to the CPU. Magnetic tapes and magnetic disks are the most common storage media. Storage is less expensive to use than memory.

Magnetic tape is a continuous plastic strip treated with an iron oxide coating that can be magnetized. It is wound onto a reel. Data is represented by magnetized spots on nine horizontal rows called tracks. EBCDIC uses eight tracks for data and the ninth for a parity bit. A tape drive has a read/write head that detects and creates the magnetized spots. Units of data called records are separated on the tape by interrecord gaps (IRGs). An IRG enables the tape to regain speed after it is stopped at the end of each record. Records can be grouped in blocks (blocked records) without IRGs to save space. They are separated by interblock gaps (IBGs).

Magnetic tapes provide for high speed transfer of large amounts of data at low cost. They are erasable and reusable, and are ideal for backup copies. They provide only sequential access to data, however, and are sensitive to environmental factors.

A magnetic disk, a direct-access medium, is a metal platter coated with a magnetizable material such as iron oxide. The surface is smooth. A read/write head stores and retrieves data in concentric circles called tracks. Disks placed on a shaft form a disk pack, in which access occurs by read/write heads on arms connected to an access mechanism. All tracks hold the same amount of data regardless of track size. Data is located on a disk by a disk address, which includes the disk surface number, track number, and record number. Records stored on disks are separated by gaps.

The floppy disk (flexible disk, diskette) is a storage medium usually used with microcomputers. Floppy disks are made of plastic, coated with a magnetizable substance. They are reusable, weigh less than 2 ounces, and are easy to store for security. A disk has a read/write notch in its jacket. While reading, the read/write head actually touches the surface of the disk.

Disks allow fast, direct access and provide quick response to inquiries. They require more complicated programming to gain access to files and to update files.

Mass storage devices provide low-cost storage used primarily for large files, backup files, and infrequently used files. Mass storage uses high-density cartridge tape and/or floppy disks.

Storage systems undergoing development include charge-coupled devices (CCD) made of silicon that are faster than bubble memory but slower than RAM, RAM disks in which RAM storage is treated as a disk drive, and laser technology. Laser storage systems use a laser that forms patterns on some type of compatible medium such as optical, or laser, disks. Compact disks are now used for storage for microcomputer systems, and include several forms: CD-ROM (read only), WORM (write-once, read-many), and erasable versions.

Superconductors are metals that are capable of transmitting high levels of current at extremely cold temperatures. Superconductors may have a major impact on technology. They may help reduce the size of supercomputers.

1. A RAM disk is a concept in which the computer treats RAM just as it does _____.
    a. a cartridge tape   c. slots
    b. a disk drive   d. data

___

c. The purpose of RAM disks is to increase the speed of access, so data that is normally accessed from disks is accessed from RAM set aside from memory or on a special circuit card.

2. In a disk pack, the top and bottom surfaces are not used for data storage because _____.
    a. they are not coated with iron oxide
    b. they do not rotate with the other platters
    c. they could become scratched or nicked thereby damaging the data
    d. the read/write arm must be placed between platters

___

c. When a disk pack contains eleven disks, for example, the top and bottom surfaces are unused, thus providing 20 instead of 22 usable surfaces.

3. A disk address is determined by _____.
    a. the amount of characters that can be placed on the particular disk
    b. the number of records and gaps placed on the disk
    c. disk surface, track, and record number
    d. the programmer who is accessing the disk

___

c. The computer can only locate data through the disk address. The address of a record is stored immediately before the record.

4. The greatest disadvantage of storage is _____.
    a. that it is slower than memory   c. it is limited to sequential-access
    b. it requires human intervention for operation d. it can only be used with magnetic tape

___

a. Storage media are not connected to the CPU. Data must be written and retrieved through the partial use of mechanical devices.

5. A WORM is a(n) _____.
   a. version of RAM disk
   b. write once, read many version of compact disk
   c. mass storage system
   d. optical disk drive

---

b. The term WORM is an acronym for write once, read many. A company can place information on the CD but once it is written, it is a permanent copy.

6. A laser storage system _____.
   a. records data by having a laser beam form patterns on a polyester sheet
   b. reads data by passing a laser beam through holes that were burned into the disk
   c. is volatile, that is, data is lost when power is disrupted
   d. is not yet practical because it deteriorates over time

---

a. The polyester sheet is coated with a thin layer of rhodium metal. Data resists alterations and provides a secure storage system.

7. The purpose of interblock gaps (IBG) on tapes is to _____.
   a. provide areas on tape to store data
   b. make data easier to find when using direct-access
   c. prevent data from being accidently erased
   d. minimize read/write operations and save space

---

d. If the records stored on a tape are very short and IRGs are long, a tape can be more than 50 percent blank, causing the tape drive to stop and accelerate constantly.

8. A disadvantage of magnetic tape is _____.
   a. it is a sequential medium   c. it is expensive
   b. it cannot be erased and reused   d. data transfer is quite slow

---

a. The entire tape must be read from beginning to end when changes are made in the data. Thus instantaneous retrieval is impossible.

9. Each track on a magnetic disk _____.
   a. stores less data towards the center of the disk because the tracks are shorter
   b. has an address directing the read/write head to the next track
   c. can store the same amount of data
   d. always has its own read/write head

---

c. Even though the tracks become smaller towards the center of the disk, each track can store the same amount of data.

10. Superconductors are _____.
   a. erasable versions of compact disks
   b. metals that can transmit high levels of current
   c. storage devices
   d. hypermedia systems

---

b. These metals are effective only in very cold environments, such as -243 degrees Fahrenheit.

❏ TRUE/FALSE

1. T F The tracks on magnetic tape extend across the width of the tape.   F

2. T F The ninth track on magnetic tape functions as a parity bit.

3. T F A read/write head creates or detects magnetized bits on tapes or disks .

4. T F Disk records do not need to be separated by gaps as tape records do.   F

5. T F The oblong opening in a diskette jacket is known as a read/write notch.

6. T F Mass storage is best used for large files, backup files, and infrequently used files.

7. T F A helium-neon laser burns a permanent hole in a tellurium film, which makes data non-erasable.

8. T F Disks are best used as sequential-access media.   F

9. T F Random-access memory (RAM) disks are the only type of storage device that can approximate the speed of a microprocessor.

10. T F An advantage of optical disks is their large storage capacity.

❏ MATCHING

a. mass storage
b. access mechanism
c. magnetic disk
d. optical disk
e. floppy disk

f. IRGs
g. RAM
h. magnetic tape
i. backup copies
j. electromagnet

i 1. One form of security for a system is making _____.

h 2. _____ is a continuous plastic strip wound on a reel.

f 3. Records are separated on tape by _____.

b 4. Read/write heads are positioned over the appropriate track by a(n) _____.

c 5. The _____ was introduced in 1973 to replace punched cards as a medium for data entry.

a 6. A low-cost method of storing vast amounts of data is called _____.

d 7. Because it can store large amounts of data, an ideal storage medium for use with a multimedia application is the _____.

g 8. The _____ disk functions like a disk, but it requires a continuous power supply for the data to be retained.

j 9. The read/write head on a tape drive is actually a(n) _____.

c 10. The metal platter coated with iron oxide and on which data is stored in concentric circles is a(n) _____.

1. What is density when referring to storage media? Compare the density of a magnetic tape with that of an optical disk.

    how closely packed the data is.

    magnetic 1600 char per inch
    optical 5000 bits of data

2. What are backup copies? Why do you think they are necessary?

    copies of files from originals or hard disk.

    in case of failure.

3. What does a cylinder shape have to do with the way data are stored in a disk pack?

    arms read each track.

4. List some advantages of magnetic disks.

   fast access
   quick response

5. Why is a cartridge tape used in mass storage better than magnetic tape?

   high density that requires less space.

6. What does a mass storage system for minicomputers use?

   floppy disks

7. Describe a charge-coupled device.

CCDS are made of Silicon + faster than bubble memory

8. Why is a helium-neon laser excellent for archival storage?

Cannot be erased

9. Why is storage necessary?

Amt of data required by program usually exceeds the capacity of memory.

10. Describe floppy disks.

3 ½
5 ¼

coated by magnatizable oxide substance

 **CHAPTER 7**

File Organization and Data Base Design

❏ KEY TERMS

Activity The proportion of records processed during an update run.

Attribute A characteristic field within a record in a computer file.

Batch file access A method of processing transactions in which transactions are accumulated for a period of time and then processed all at once.

Data base Collection of data that is commonly defined and consistently organized to fit the information needs of a wide variety of users in an organization.

Data base management system (DBMS) A set of programs that serves as the interface between the data base and the programmer, operating system, and users; also programs used to design and maintain data bases.

Data structure A particular relationship between the data elements in a computer file.

Direct-access file design A file design in which records are organized in a file in any order, with key fields providing the only way to access data; must be used with direct-access storage.

Direct-access storage device (DASD) Auxiliary storage device that allows data to be stored and accessed either randomly or sequentially.

Directory A computerized list that contains record keys and their corresponding addresses; used to obtain the address of a record with a direct-access file design.

Hierarchical structure Also called tree structure; the data structure in which one primary element may have numerous secondary elements linked to it at lower levels.

Indexed-sequential file design A file design in which records are organized sequentially and also listed in an index, which allows for both sequential and direct-access processing.

Inverted structure A data structure that indexes a simple file by specific record attributes.

Key The unique identifier or field of a record; used to sort records for processing or to locate specific records within a file.

Key value A value used to arrange records within a data file or data base.

Linear structure A data structure in which the records in a computer file are arranged sequentially in a specified order.

Logical file The combination of data used to meet a user's need.

Master file A file that contains all existing records organized according to the key field; updated by records in a transaction file.

Network structure The data structure in which a primary data element may have many secondary elements linked to it and any given secondary element may be linked to numerous primary elements.

Online file access An access method that provides the ability to retrieve current information at any time; when a transaction is created, related information is updated simultaneously.

Physical file The way data is stored by the computer.

Primary key A unique field for a record; used to sort records for processing or to locate a particular record within a file.

Randomizing (hashing) A mathematical process applied to the record key that produces the storage address of the record.

Relational structure The data structure that places the data elements in a table with rows representing records and columns representing fields.

Secondary key A field used to gain access to records on a file; may not be a unique identifier.

Sequential file design A file design in which records are organized in a file in a specific order based on the value of the key field.

Sequential processing The process of creating a new master file each time transactions are processed; requires batch file access.

Simple structure Data structure in which records in a computer file are arranged sequentially.

Transaction file A file containing changes to be made to the master file.

Volatility The frequency of changes made to a file during a certain period of time.

❑ SUMMARY

File processing is the activity of updating permanent files to reflect the effects of changes in data, with or without a computerized system. Many companies can save time and money by computerizing file processing activities.

Two considerations in determining the best file design for an organization are how quickly the data must be processed and the manner in which data will be retrieved. Two access methods are possible: batch and online. In batch file access, all transactions to be processed are gathered for a logical time period and processed all at once. Batch processing is most useful when information is needed only at set times. Online file access enables the user to get information at any time. Each time a transaction occurs, affected records are updated at the same time.

Different access methods require different file designs. Sequential file design is best for batch file access. Direct-access and indexed-sequential file designs are best for online access.

In sequential file design, records are arranged according to a key value. The key is one data field chosen to identify the record. The key must be unique. Updating requires two files: master and transaction. The master file contains all existing records in sequential order. The transaction file contains the changes to be made to the master file. A new master is created during the update. The records may be added, changed, or deleted during sequential processing. Old files called "father" and "grandfather" are retained to recreate files in case new files are destroyed.

Sequential processing and file design are best for high activity and low volatility files. Activity is the portion of records processed during an update. Volatility is the frequency of changes to a file during a given time period.

Direct-access file design uses the key field to access data within a direct-access design. Records are not stored in any particular order. A data record is retrieved according to its key value. A mathematical process called randomizing, or hashing, is applied to the key. The result is the record's address. Another way to retrieve data requires the use of a directory containing the record's address and data keys. Direct-access is efficient when information must be updated and retrieved quickly. Direct-access storage devices (DASDs) make this processing possible.

Direct-access processing and file design are suitable for applications with low activity and high volatility. Files can be updated without first being sorted. Access requires only a fraction of a second. Unlike sequential processing, with direct-access processing the master is updated directly; thus, no old master remains.

Indexed-sequential file design is for applications in which activity and volatility are both high. Records are stored sequentially using a primary key. Secondary keys, fields similar to primary keys but not unique, may be used along with the primary keys. Records can be accessed randomly via the primary and secondary key or read sequentially. An index table is created with an address referring to several grouped records. In secondary key access, the system locates the address and then reads sequentially until the primary key record is found. Access time is faster than sequential access but slower than direct access.

A data base approach treats all data from every department as one entity. A data base is a single collection of related data stored on a direct-access device. Data duplication is minimized. Data bases are very efficient. Data updated in one area updates all areas at once. Data-base systems depend on DASDs to allow easy retrieval of data items.

The system analyst and the data-base analyst determine the design of data in a data base. (The system analyst is the interface between users and system programmers. The data base analyst designs and implements the data base.) A good data base incorporates several physical files into one logical file. Ways in which data can logically be joined together are called data structures. The most common are simple, hierarchical, network, and relational.

Simple structure is a sequential arrangement of records. Each record has fields called attributes. The linear structure contains records that are ordered or arranged in a specific sequence. An inverted structure contains indexes for selected attributes in a file.

A hierarchical (tree) structure has many data elements linked at various levels. The primary element is the parent. Each parent may have several secondary (child) elements. Each child is allowed only one parent.

The network structure is similar to hierarchical, but a child data element may have more than one parent. Any data element may be linked to any other.

The relational structure places the data elements in a table with rows and columns. Subscripts are used to locate a particular row and column juncture. This type of data structure is considered more user-friendly than the others.

A data base management system (DBMS) is a set of programs that serves as an interface between the data base and programmer, operating system, and user.

❏ STRUCTURED LEARNING

1. Batch file access is most useful _____.
    a. when the files are processed frequently
    b. when current information is needed at set times
    c. in processing low activity files
    d. in processing high volatility files

---

b.   The transactions are gathered for a certain period of time and then processed all at once.

2. In sequential files, records are found by arranging them _____.
   a. according to a key value
   b. in the order they were received
   c. with most frequently accessed records at the beginning
   d. no particular order is necessary in sequential files since all must be accessed anyway

---

a. The key is one data field chosen to identify the record. The key must be unique.

3. One way of obtaining the address of a record in direct-access file design is _____.
   a. to place the record key and address in a directory
   b. to create a separate file containing record addresses
   c. by sorting all records prior to storage
   d. by using "father" and "grandfather" files

---

a. When using a directory, the computer searches the directory for the key and uses the corresponding address to locate the record.

4. A data-base approach to file design _____.
   a. involves a great deal of data duplication to accomplish
   b. cannot be used with online processing
   c. treats all data from every department as one entity
   d. is a very secure method of data storage

---

c. A data base minimizes the duplication of data. It is a single collection of data that can be used for many applications.

5. Types of data structures are _____.
   a. simple, hierarchical, network, and relational   c. logical, physical, and complex
   b. simple, complex, double, and triple   d. linear, logical, and inverted

---

a. Data elements in a file can be arranged according to how they are related to one another. These are ways in which data elements can be joined logically.

6. The newest type of data base is the _____.
   a. hierarchical
   b. tree
   c. relational
   d. network

---

c. Relational data bases were developed to provide a more user-friendly approach to data base accessing.

7. Without computers, file processing _____.
   a. is called bookkeeping
   b. must be done on paper, manually
   c. is impossible
   d. requires more frequent updating

---

b. File processing is the activity of updating permanent files to reflect changes in data.

8. In determining the best file design for an organization, an important consideration is the _____.
   a. manner in which data will be retrieved
   b. types of data to be stored
   c. key field
   d. amount of data in a record

---

a. There are two access methods, batch or online, depending on how fast data must be retrieved.

9. Updating a sequential file involves two files; they are _____.
   a. master file and update file
   b. father and grandfather files
   c. new file and old file
   d. transaction file and master file

---

d. The master file contains all existing records. The transaction file contains the changes to be made to the master.

10. Backup "father" and "grandfather" files _____.
    a. are sent to the IRS
    b. are kept for security reasons
    c. serve no useful purpose, they are simply left over from file updates
    d. are sequential-access files converted to direct-access files

---

b. The old master and transaction are kept for a period of time. In the event later masters are lost or destroyed, they can be recreated.

1. T F A direct-access system does not require transaction records to be sorted before processing.

2. T F After sequential-access files are updated, the old master is called the "father" file.

3. T F Secondary keys in indexed-sequential files must be unique.

4. T F An advantage of indexed-sequential files is that access is faster than direct-access.

5. T F Records in indexed-sequential files can be grouped together and one address given to the entire group.

6. T F An index table lists the names of the files in a data base.

7. T F The activity of a sequential-access file is low.

8. T F Sequential-access file design is best suited to inquiry-and-response applications.

9. T F When records are ordered according to their key values, a sequential file is formed.

10. T F Three possible operations in updating a file are add, change, and delete.

❑ **MATCHING**

a. system analyst   f. DASD
b. secondary key   g. hierarchical
c. sequential processing   h. online file access
d. data-base analyst   i. hashing
e. primary key   j. network

1. The process that creates an entirely new master file each time transactions are processed is called _____.

2. Another word for randomizing to obtain an address is _____.

3. A device, such as a magnetic-disk drive, used to store data using an online-access method is a(n) _____.

4. A field that contains unique data can be a(n) _____.

5. A data structure in which data elements are linked so that a parent can have many children, but each child may have only one parent is a(n) _____ structure.

6. A field that is used to gain access to records on the file, but need not be unique is a(n) _____.

7. A data structure in which any data element can be related to any other element is a(n) _____ structure.

8. The interface between users and system programmers in a data base system is the _____.

9. The ability to retrieve current information at any time is provided by _____.

10. The _____ is responsible for the analysis, design, and implementation of the data base.

❏ SHORT ANSWER

1. What is a data-base management system (DBMS)?

2. Name three file designs.

3. List three advantages of data bases.

4. Explain the difference between activity and volatility.

5. Name two advantages of sequential processing.

6. Describe the relational data structure.

7. What is a simple data structure?

8. List three advantages of direct-access processing and file design.

9. Explain an inverted structure.

10. List two advantages of indexed-sequential files.

 **CHAPTER 8**

Microcomputers

❏ KEY TERMS

Application   Also application program; a set of instructions written to solve a specific user problem.

Boot   To load the start-up instructions into the computer's memory.

Command-line user interface   A user interface that, by design, requires the user to type in commands that are then executed by the computer's operating system.

Compatible   Descriptive of hardware or software produced by one manufacturer to be used on computers or with software produced by another manufacturer.

Desktop   A metaphor for the user's working environment in the Macintosh user interface or in any graphical user interface, such as Microsoft Windows.

Document   A file that contains information entered into the computer by the user.

Finder   The portion of the Macintosh operating system that displays the desktop and manages the data and information stored on disk.

Folder   A device on the desktop that can hold documents, applications, and other folders, a tool used to organize the desktop

Graphical user interface (GUI)   A user interface to the computer's operating system that uses graphics, or pictures, and menus to simplify the user's task of working with the computer.

Icon   A graphic, or picture, used to represent such things as an application, document, folder, or disk on the Macintosh desktop and other graphical user interfaces.

Instruction set   The fundamental logical and arithmetic procedures that the computer can perform, such as addition, subtraction, and comparison.

Laptop portable   A small microcomputer that is powered by a rechargeable battery, weighs between eight and twelve pounds, and has a hard disk and a 3 1/2-inch floppy disk drive.

Modem   Also called a data set; a device that modulates and demodulates signals transmitted over communication facilities.

MS-DOS   The disk operating system used on IBM PCs and compatible computers.

Notebook portable   The smallest microcomputer available; weighs less than eight pounds, has a hard disk and one 3 1/2-inch floppy disk drive, and operates on rechargeable batteries.

Path   A way in which the user can indicate to the MS-DOS (or PC-DOS) operating system where a file is located on a disk. The path may include directory names as well as file names.

PC-DOS   The disk operating system used on IBM personal computers.

Portable computer   A small microcomputer weighing between twelve and seventeen pounds; runs on rechargeable betteries and usually has a hard disk and a 3 1/2-inch floppy disk drive.

Prompt   A message or cue that guides the user; it indicates to the user what type of input is required or what might be wrong in the case of an error.

Root directory   In the MS-DOS or PC-DOS operating system, the directory created by default when a floppy disk or hard disk is formatted. There can be only one root directory per disk.

Subdirectory   In the MS-DOS and PC-DOS operating systems, a subdirectory is an extension of the root directory.

Supermicrocomputer   A microcomputer built around a 32-bit microprocessor and powerful enough to compete with low-end minicomputers.

Transparent user interface   An operating system that reduces the amount of knowledge required by the user.

Transportable computer   A computer that weighs more than 17 pounds, but is still small enough to be carried; requires an external power source; contains a hard disk drive and is normally comparable in power to a desktop microcomputer.

Users group   An informal group of owners of a particular microcomputer or software package who meet to exchange information about hardware, software, service, and support.

Working directory   The directory in which the user is located on either a floppy disk or a hard disk in the MS-DOS or PC-DOS operating system.

❏ SUMMARY

The microcomputer (also personal computer, home computer) is the smallest computer. Some are called supermicrocomputers. Most can sit on a desktop. The CPU of a microcomputer is the microprocessor, which is much miniaturized compared with the first one developed by Ted Hoff at Intel. The instructions used for arithmetic, logic operations, and storage and retrieval operations are designed into the chip and are called its instruction set. A recent development, the Reduced Instruction Set Computer (RISC), uses a simple and small set of instructions, down from the some 300 instructions on 32-bit microprocessors.

The operating systems of microcomputers are usually less complex and less expensive than those of larger computers, but the prefix micro applies more to size and cost than to capability.

Most desktop microcomputers are equipped with a keyboard, disk drive, monitor, and printer. The main system board (mother board) holds the microprocessor, other circuits, and memory chips. The system board often contains slots in which to insert cards that expand the capabilities of the machine. The ports are used for plugging in peripherals.

Although most microcomputers are desktop models, there are two other groups: portables and supermicrocomputers. The division portables has four subdivisions: notebooks, laptops, portables, and transportables. All, normally excepting transportables, operate with rechargeable batteries. Portables are distinguished by their flat screen displays. Supermicrocomputers have 32-bit microprocessors and compete with small minicomputers.

An operating system is a set of programs that provide an interface between the user or applications program and the computer hardware. A computer automatically loads (boots) the operating system from disk when the computer is turned on. Operating systems have varying levels of versatility, ease of use, and sophistication. Control program for microprocessors (CP/M) was the first operating system for 8-bit microcomputers. MS-DOS was later written and has become the most popular 16-bit operating system. The Apple computer uses a simple Apple DOS and the updated ProDOS.

The user must have a way to communicate with the operating system to tell the computer what to do. One method is through a command-line user interface, which requires the user to type codes for the commands. An example is MS-DOS. MS-DOS and PC-DOS have two basic types of files_executable (program files and batch files) and data files. Each file has a unique name consisting of the file name and the file name extension. A fully qualified filename also includes the path name. The files are organized in directories, one of which is the root directory created by default when a disk is formatted. The subdirectory is created as an extension to the root directory. The directory in which a user is working is the working directory.

Another method of communicating with the operating system is through a transparent user interface, which requires less knowledge. The transparent user interfaces, often called graphical user interfaces

(GUIs), enable the user to point to icons and use pull-menus to issue commands. A mouse is often used with GUIs. The Macintosh Finder is an example. A Macintosh user communicates by using the icons and pull-down menus located on the desktop.

A software package is a set of standardized computer programs that solve problems of a specific application. The "big four" packages normally used for business are word processing, electronic spreadsheets, data-base manager, and graphics. Two or more of these packages, or enhancements to one package, may be integrated, or blended, into one package.

Software, computers, and peripherals must be compatible in order for a task to be accomplished. This means that one manufacturer's equipment or software can be used with another manufacturer's equipment or software.

Users of microcomputers often form users groups, which are informal groups who exchange information about hardware, software, service, and support. They may own a particular computer model or software package or be interested in a particular topic.

Before buying a microcomputer, the prospective owner should first decide what jobs need to be done and select the software that will be required. The user should learn about the software and test the software for hardware requirements, flexibility, organization, error handling, data requirements, command styles, help screens, copy protection, vendor policies, macros, and defaults. The hardware should be matched to the software and job. Hardware can be bought from microcomputer vendors, retailers, and mail-order houses. Before purchasing hardware, the user should evaluate the microprocessor, monitors, keyboards, storage, printers, and other add-on devices. Training for using the hardware and software is available from seminars by manufacturers and dealers, college and high school classes, users groups, and self study.

❏ STRUCTURED LEARNING

1. Supermicrocomputers are built around powerful 32-bit microprocessors, _____.
    a. and may have multiple processors
    b. and run on battery power
    c. but support only one user
    d. and are actually a subset of minicomputers

---

a. Supermicrocomputers do not run on battery power, and may support more than one user. They are microcomputers, not minicomputers.

2. Features characteristic of graphical user interfaces include the use of _____.
    a. prompts   c. mice and hard disk drives
    b. applications and documents   d. icons and pull-down menus

d. Graphical user interfaces are based on visual cues such as pictures, or icons, that the user uses to command the computer.

3. Files in MS-DOS and PC-DOS are identified by _____.
    a. file names and file name extensions   c. directories
    b. icons   d. addresses

a. Each file has a name that includes a file name and a file name extension. A fully qualified file name also includes the path name.

4. The motherboard in a microcomputer is _____.
    a. a slot   c. the main system board
    b. the desktop   d. a memory card

c. The motherboard holds the microprocessor, other circuits, and memory chips. It may contain slots for plugging in cards for adding memory.

5. Transportable microcomputers _____.
    a. are powered by batteries
    b. require an external power source
    c. are divided by size into briefcase, notebook, and handheld
    d. are those under 17 pounds

b. Transportables are generally larger than portables, but are still small enough to be carried and require an external power source.

6. RISC technology _____ than traditional design.
    a. uses more space on microprocessor
    b. makes more efficient use of space on a microprocessor
    c. makes more efficient use of space on the main system board
    d. makes more use of parallel processing

d. The acronym RISC stands for reduced instruction set computer, and was developed because traditional instruction set design was using too much space on the microprocessor.

7. A term that refers to the less a user needs to know about an operating system and the less the system is noticed is _____.

    a. compatible   c. translucent

    b. transparent   d. pictorial

---

b. While a transparent operating system may be less confusing, it may offer less flexibility in customizing a computer system.

8. Integrated software is software that _____.

    a. can be used on a wide variety of computer systems

    b. is sold with a great deal of vendor support

    c. is a blend of two or more applications normally sold as separate software packages

    d. contains a wide variety of defaults

---

c. Integrated software may contain several unrelated applications such as word processing, electronic spreadsheets, and file handlers or it may consist of a main package and its enhancements, such as word processing with a thesaurus and a grammar checker.

9. The ability to use one manufacturer's equipment or software with that of another manufacturer is referred to as _____.

    a. user friendliness   c. networking

    b. compatibility   d. transparency

---

b. Compatibility can be extended by adding another microprocessor to a computer. The second microprocessor makes the computer compatible with another operating system.

10. You should consider error handling, command styles, macros, and defaults when buying _____.

    a. software   c. printers

    b. microprocessors   d. add-ons

---

a. The characteristics listed describe aspects of software.

❏ TRUE/FALSE

1. T F Large microcomputers are called supermicrocomputers.

2. T F The primary development that led to today's microprocessor was the miniaturization of circuits.

3. T F The instruction set is another name for the operating system. F

4. T F Laptop computers run on battery power and have hard disk drives and flat-panel displays.

5. T F Some portable computers also include modems and built-in languages such as BASIC.

6. T F A port may be designed for serial communication or parallel processing. F

7. T F The program Microsoft Windows provides a transparent user interface.

8. T F Pointers in the Macintosh user interface include applications, documents, and folders. F

9. T F The root directory is created by default when a disk is formatted.

10. T F Ports and slots are two names for the same feature of computers. F

❏ MATCHING

a. icon   f. mouse
b. CP/M   g. notebooks
c. transparent   h. MS-DOS
d. default   i. instruction set
e. RGB   j. macro

g 1. The smallest microcomputers are _____.

j 2. A command used to define several keys or key commands as a single key is a(n) _____.

i 3. Functions designed into a microcomputer's circuitry for arithmetic and logic and storage and retrieval functions are the _____.

b 4. The first operating system for microcomputers was _____.

h 5. The operating system for 16-bit microcomputers that has become very popular is _____.

a 6. A picture representation or graphic image that appears on the computer screen is called a(n) _____.

7. A device that is rolled on a surface and used to control the position of the cursor or enter a command is the _____.

8. Monitors that receive three separate color signals are _____ monitors.

9. Operating systems that require the user to have little knowledge of the operating system are described as _____.

10. Values that the computer assumes when the user does not state new values are _____ values.

❑ SHORT ANSWER

1. Describe the purpose of slots. How do they differ from ports?

   Slots are positions on the motherboard to place add-ons

   ports are outlets plugs

2. Name some common uses of microprocessors other than microcomputers.

   microwaves
   calculators
   Sewing machines

3. In PC-DOS and MS-DOS, what is the working directory?

the directory you are in

4. Name three major groups of microcomputers. Explain the difference between a portable and a transportable.

Portable

desktop

Supermicro

portable- can be battery operated, smaller

5. List three types of portables.

laptop
transportable
notebook

6. Name three technologies that are normally found in laptop computers.

battery operated

flat screen

micro processors

7. Explain the term "booting."

a small program in ROM starts loading the machine when the computer is turned on

8. What is a transparent operating system?

lessens the amount of knowledge required by user.

icons + pull down menu

9. Define compatibility and explain how a coprocessor extends compatibility.

— to use another vendors product

— coprocessor can make the computer compatible
/another operating system.

10. List the four software packages often seen as filling the needs of four basic tasks in business.

w..p.
spreadsheet
graphics
database

CHAPTER 9

Telecommunications and Networks

❑ KEY TERMS

Acoustic-coupler modem   A device used in telecommunications that is attached to a computer by a cable and that connects to a standard telephone handset.

Analog transmission   Transmission of data over communication channels in a continuous wave form.

Automatic teller machine (ATM)   Remote terminal that allows bank customers to make transactions with the bank's central computer; users can check account balances, transfer funds, make deposits and withdrawals, pay on loans, and so forth.

Bandwidth   Also known as grade; the range of width of the frequencies available for transmission on a given channel.

Broad-band channel   A communication channel that can transmit data at rates of up to 120,000 bits per second; for example, microwaves.

Buffer   A separate area of memory in which characters can be stored and retrieved; used when transmitting data from one device to another.

Bus configuration   A network design used with local area networks (LANs) in which multiple stations connected to a communication cable can communicate directly with any other station on the line.

Channel   A limited-capacity computer that takes over the tasks of input and output in order to free the CPU to handle internal processing operations.

Communication channel   A medium for carrying data from one location to another.

Concentrator   A device that systematically allocates the use of communication channels among several terminals.

Data buffering   Reading data into a separate storage unit normally contained in the control unit of the input/output system.

Datacom handler   Another name for multiplexer and concentrator.

Data communication   The electronic transmission of data from one site to another, usually over communication channels such as telephone lines or microwaves.

Demodulation   The process of retrieving data from a modulated carrier wave.

Digital transmission   The transmission of data as distinct on and off pulses.

Direct-connect modem   A device used in telecommunications that is attached to a computer by a cable and that connects directly to a telephone line by plugging into a standard phone jack.

Distributed computing (distributed data processing)   A system in which data processing is done at a site other than that of the central computer.

Electronic funds transfer (EFT)   A cashless method of managing money; accounts involved in a transaction are adjusted by electronic communications between computers.

Electronic mail   Transmission of messages at high speeds over telecommunication facilities.

File server   The portion of a local-area network (LAN) that allows for the sharing of peripheral devices and information.

Front-end processor   A small CPU serving as an interface between a large CPU and peripheral devices.

Fully distributed configuration   A network design in which every set of nodes in the network can communicate directly with every other set of nodes through a single communication link.

Grade   See Bandwidth.

Hierarchical configuration   A network design for multiple CPUs in which an organization's needs are divided into multiple levels that receive different levels of computer support.

In-house   An organization's use of its own personnel or resources to develop programs or other problem-solving systems.

Input/output bound   A situation in which the CPU is slowed down because of I/O operations, which are extremely slow in comparison to CPU internal processing speeds.

Input/output control unit   A device located between one or more I/O devices that performs code conversion.

Internal modem   A modem that plugs into the internal circuitry of a computer; no external cables or connections are needed.

Link   A transmission channel that connects modes.

Local system   Peripherals connected directly to the CPU.

Local-area network (LAN)   A way of connecting microcomputers together for the sharing of peripheral devices and information and for communication among members of the network.

Message switching   The task of a communications processor of receiving messages and routing them to appropriate destinations.

Modem (data set)   A device that modulates and demodulates signals transmitted over communication lines.

Modulation   A technology used in modems to make data processing signals compatible with communication facilities.

Multiplexer   A device that permits more than one I/O device to transmit data over the same communication channel.

Narrow bandwidth channel   A communication channel that can transmit data only at a rate between 45 to 90 bits per second_for example, telegraph channels.

Network   The linking together of multiple CPUs.

Network interface card (NIC)   An integrated circuit board that is plugged into the circuitry of each microcomputer on a local-area network (LAN); enables the members of the network to communicate with each other.

Network operating system (NOS)   The computer software that controls the use of the local-area network (LAN) by its members.

Node   The endpoint of a network, e.g., CPUs, printers, CRTs, or other physical devices.

Poll   The process used by a concentrator to determine if an input/output device is ready to send a message to the CPU.

Programmable communications processor   A device that relieves the CPU of the task of monitoring data transmission.

Protocol   The description of rules of communication when transmitting and receiving data on a network.

Remote system A system in which terminals are connected to the central computer by a communication channel.

Ring configuration A network design in which a number of computers are connected by a single transmission line in a ring formation.

Selector channel A channel that can accept input from only one device at a time; generally used with high-speed I/O devices such as magnetic tape or magnetic disk units.

Star configuration A network design in which all transactions must go through a central computer before being routed to the appropriate network computer.

Telecommunication The combined use of communication facilities, such as telephone systems and data-processing equipment.

Telecommuting Method of working at home by communicating via electronic machines and telecommunication facilities.

Time-sharing system An arrangement in which two or more users can access the same central computer resources and receive what seems to be simultaneous results.

Time slicing A technique used in a time-sharing system that allocates a small portion of processing time to each user.

Voice-grade channel A communication channel that has a wider frequency range and can transmit data at a rate between 300 and 9,600 bits per second; for example, a telephone line.

Workstation A member of a local-area network (LAN) where work on applications takes place.

❑ SUMMARY

Data communication is the electronic transmission of data from one location to another, usually over communication channels such as telephone lines or microwaves. The combined use of communication facilities and data-processing equipment is called telecommunication.

A communication channel is the link that permits transmission of electrical signals between distributed data processing (DDP) locations. Types of media used as communication channels are telephone lines, coaxial cables, fiber-optic cables, and microwaves. Channels are classified by grade, or bandwidth, which determines the range of frequency at which it can transmit data. Three grades are narrow bandwidth, voice-grade, and broad-band. Communication channels operate in one of three basic transmission modes: simple, half-duplex, and full-duplex.

Data can be transmitted in one of two forms: continuous wave form (analog transmission) and on and off pulses (digital transmission). In order for digital data to be carried by analog transmission, it must be modulated, or converted from pulse form to wave form. Demodulation is the process of converting the wave form to pulse form. The conversion is done by devices called modems, or data sets. Three types of modems are acoustic-coupler modem, direct-connect modem, and internal modem.

Communication occurs between the computer and peripheral devices, also. This is usually dictated by commands a human enters through a computer terminal. Input/output (I/O) devices convert this data to machine-readable form. The code conversion specifically occurs in the input/output (I/O) control unit, a unit located between one or more I/O devices and the CPU. (It is not the same as the control unit in the CPU.) I/O control units also perform data buffering. A buffer is a temporary storage unit that allows a large quantity of data to be transferred faster than individual data items.

I/O device speeds are very slow, so when the CPU slows to wait for data transfer, it is said to be input/output bound. To increase the use of the CPU, channels are used to take over the job of transferring data to and from the CPU. Three types of channels, or datacom handlers, are concentrator, multiplexer, and selector. They allow multiple I/O devices to share one communication channel. A multiplexer acts by combining several input streams from devices into one single stream and sending the stream over a single channel. A concentrator checks or polls several terminals until it finds a terminal with a signal to send. It can handle data from only one terminal at a time. A selector can also only accept input from one device at a time. It is often used for specialized high-speed jobs. Another device that takes over from the CPU many tasks involved in communication is the programmable communications processor. Two frequent uses are message switching and front-end processing.

A computer network is the linking together of CPUs and terminals via a communication system. This allows users to share files, devices, and programs. Single and multiple CPU networks are used.

A single CPU network consists of one mainframe linked to many peripherals. Peripherals connected directly to the CPU form a local system. A remote system has the CPU and peripherals connected through a communication channel. Organizations that only occasionally need a large computer can use a single CPU network called a time-sharing system. The computer time is divided among several users in a technique known a time slicing, which allocates to each user small portions of processing time. The system rotates among these small slices of time at such a rapid pace that the user never notices. Time sharing can occur in-house or by purchasing time from a service company.

Multiple CPU networks consist of two structures: nodes and links. A node is an end point of a system such as a CPU, printer, and terminal. Links are the transmission channels that connect the nodes. Nodes and links can be arranged in several types of configurations, or topologies. The most common are star, ring, hierarchical, bus, and fully distributed.

Local-area networks are networks used to link multiple microcomputers for sharing peripherals and information. LANs operate within a well-defined, self-enclosed area. The communication stations are linked by cable and are usually within 1,000 feet. The members of a LAN are the file server, which allows for this sharing, and the workstations, or computers where users work. Each member has a network interface card (NIC) that allows it to communicate with other members. The software that controls network operations is called the network operating system (NOS).

Standards set by government agencies and leading companies within the telecommunication industry enable transmission in a consistent fashion. Thus, telecommunication can be used for a number of practical jobs—for example, banking, telecommuting, and telecomputing. Banks make use of electronic funds transfer (EFT) by adjusting the accounts of parties involved in a transaction. No cash or checks are used. Automatic Teller Machines (ATM) enable customers to access their accounts through unattended remote devices. Some banks are beginning use of a "smart" card, which is similar to a credit card with an imbedded microchip.

Telecommuting allows employees to work at home using a computer rather than commute to an office.

Information services, or commercial data bases, allow personal computers to access vast banks of information that are stored on a central computer system. This is often called telecomputing. Information services such as CompuServe, The Source, and Dow Jones News/Retrieval offer a variety of information. Bulletin boards provide an informal way for users to post notices and communicate with each other.

❏ STRUCTURED LEARNING

1. The combined use of communication facilities, such as telephone systems, and data-processing equipment is called _____.
   - a. data distribution
   - b. telecommunication
   - c. telecomputing
   - d. information transmission

b. The communication network provides the means for the input and output devices to communicate with both themselves and the computer tied to the network.

2. A temporary holding area between the CPU and an I/O device is a _____.
   - a. buffer
   - b. modem
   - c. demodulator
   - d. data storage unit

a. The buffer allows a large quantity of data to be transferred much faster than if the data items were transferred individually.

3. A CPU is input/output bound when _____.
   a. too much data is transferred at once
   b. a multiplexer fails
   c. too many channels are in use at one time
   d. the CPU slows to wait for I/O operations

---

d. Compared with the CPUs internal processing speed, I/O speeds are extremely slow. Even high-speed I/Os work only 1/10th as fast as the CPU.

4. An advantage of fiber optics as a channel is that _____.
   a. the cable allows signals to bend
   b. the cable is a broad-band channel
   c. the signal is in analog form
   d. there is reduced chance for errors

---

d. Light impulses (laser beams) are sent along clear, flexible tubing approximately half the diameter of a human hair in digital form, thus because there is no need for conversion to analog form, transmission is more accurate.

5. A half-duplex channel transmission mode enables _____.
   a. data to flow in two directions, but only one way at a time
   b. data to flow only one way
   c. data to flow in both directions simultaneously
   d. digital transmission only

---

a. Modems capable of half-duplex transmission are commonly used in telephone services and networks.

6. Multiplexers and concentrators are also known as _____.
   a. selectors
   b. message switchers
   c. datacom handlers
   d. programmable communications processors

---

c. They increase the number of I/O devices that can use a communication channel.

7. A device that relieves the CPU of many communication tasks is a _____.
   a. local-area network   c. communications buffer
   b. programmable communications processor   d. data concentrator

---

b. When the volume of data transmission surpasses a certain level, a programmable communications processor can handle these tasks more economically than the CPU.

8. In banking, the main function of electronic funds transfer (EFT) is _____.
   a. banks only to conduct electronic transactions
   b. telecommuting
   c. a customer to use a credit card
   d. banking to occur with no exchange of cash or checks

---

d. The accounts of a party or parties involved in a transaction are adjusted by electronic communication between computers.

9. Some employees don't like telecommuting because _____.
   a. their phone bills are increased
   b. fraud is more likely
   c. "out of sight is out of mind"
   d. it enables them to work at home if they have children

---

c. Some employees fear that if a manager does not see them work, they will be passed over when promotions and raises are considered.

10. The multiple network configuration that has single-point vulnerability is _____.
    a. star   c. bus
    b. ring   d. hierarchical

---

a. All transactions must go through a central computer before being routed to the appropriate computer. When the central computer breaks down, all nodes in the network are disabled.

TRUE/FALSE

1. T F A communication channel permits transmission of data between distributed data processing locations.

2. T F A direct-connect modem is a circuit board that is plugged into the internal circuitry of the computer terminal.

3. T F Analog transmission of data tends to be faster and more accurate than digital transmission.

4. T F If the CPU executes an instruction that requires input or output, it must wait for data to be moved.

5. T F Ordinary telephones use copper wire in data transmission because it is an excellent conductor of electricity.

6. T F Microwave transmission occurs at high speeds and offers flexibility because there is no physical link between transmission points.

7. T F Full-duplex transmission is the most versatile type of transmission available.

8. T F The grade or bandwidth of a channel determines the range of frequency at which it can transmit data.

9. T F When peripherals are connected directly to the CPU, the system is called a local system.

10. T F A disadvantage of time-sharing is that there may be a problem with security.

MATCHING

a. I/O control unit
b. node
c. channel
d. protocol
e. automatic teller machine
f. fully distributed
g. data communication
h. broad-band
i. file server
j. grade

1. _____ is the electronic transmission of data from one location to another over communication channels.

2. The member of a LAN that enables the sharing of peripheral devices and information is the _____.

3. A description of rules of communication to be used when sending and receiving data on a network is the _____.

4. Code conversion is performed by the _____, which is located between an I/O device and the CPU.

5. To increase use of the CPU, a(n) _____ can take over the task of transferring data to and from the CPU.

6. Communication channels that can transmit data at a rate of up to 120,000 bits per second are _____ channels.

7. The _____ or bandwidth of a channel determines the range of frequency at which it can transmit data.

8. An unattended remote device used in banking is a(n) _____.

9. A configuration in which every set of nodes in a network can communicate with the other sets of nodes, but also has its own processing capabilities is a(n) _____ configuration.

10. A(n) _____ is an end point of a network.

❏ SHORT ANSWER

1. What are the three types of modems?

2. What is the derivation of the word modem?

3. Explain the difference between a concentrator channel and a multiplexer channel.

4. Name the four most common communication channels for data transfer.

5. What are the three grade classifications of channels?

6. Explain the three transmission modes of channels.

7. When a concentrator polls the terminals for data to send, what assumption is being made?

8. What are the two most frequent uses of communications processors?

9. List three advantages of time-sharing.

10. Name some of the more common types of multiple CPU network configurations.

 **CHAPTER 10**

System Software

Application program   A sequence of instructions written to solve a specific user problem.

Back-end processor   A small CPU serving as an interface between a large CPU and a large data base stored on a direct-access storage device.

Concurrently Taking place within the same time interval. In multiprogramming, concurrent processing occurs when the processing alternates between different programs.

Control program   A routine, usually part of an operating system, that aids in controlling the operations and management of a computer system.

Front-end processor   A small CPU serving as an interface between a large CPU and peripheral devices.

Input/output management system   A subsystem of the operating system that controls and coordinates the CPU while receiving input from channels, executing instructions of programs in memory, and regulating output.

Interrupt   A condition or event that temporarily suspends normal processing operations.

Job control language (JCL) A language that serves as the communication link between the programmer and the computer operating system.

Job control program   A control program that translates the job-control statements written by a programmer into machine-language instructions that can be executed by the computer.

Memory management/memory protection   In a multiprogramming environment, the process of keeping the programs in memory separate from each other.

Multiprocessing A multiple CPU configuration in which jobs are processed simultaneously.

Multiprogramming The process of executing multiple programs concurrently; the CPU switches from one program to another so quickly that program execution seems to be simultaneous.

Multitasking Running two or more programs on a computer at once.

Operating system   A collection of programs designed to permit a computer system to manage itself and to avoid idle CPU time while increasing utilization of computer resources.

Page   Material that fits in one page frame of memory.

Page frame   In a virtual memory environment, one of the fixed-sized physical areas into which memory is divided.

Paging   A method of implementing virtual memory: data and programs are broken into fixed-sized blocks, or pages, and loaded into memory when needed during processing.

Processing program   A routine, usually part of an operating system, that is used to simplify program preparation and execution.

Real memory   Primary memory; contrast with virtual memory.

Region   In multiprogramming with a variable number of tasks, a term often used to mean the internal space allocated for a particular program; a variable-sized partition.

Resident routine   A frequently used component of the supervisor that is initially loaded into memory.

Segment   A variable-sized block or portion of a program used in a virtual memory system.

Segmentation   A method of implementing virtual memory; involves dividing a program into variable-sized blocks, called segments, depending on the program logic.

Serial processing   A method of processing in which programs are executed one at a time; usually found in simple operating systems, such as those used on the earliest computer systems.

Sort/merge program   A type of operating system utility program used to sort records to facilitate updating and subsequent combining of files to form a single, updated file.

Subroutine   A set of statements not within the main line of the program; saves the programmer time by not having to write the same instructions over again in different parts of the program.

Supervisor program (monitor, executive)   The major component of the operating system; coordinates the activities of all other parts of the operating system.

Swapping   In a virtual memory environment, the process of transferring a program section from virtual memory to real memory, and vice versa.

System program   A program that coordinates the operation of computer circuitry and assists in the development of application programs. System programs are designed to facilitate the efficient use of the computer's resources.

System residence device   An storage device (disk, tape, or drum) on which operating-system programs are stored and from which they are loaded into memory.

Thrashing   Programs in which little actual processing occurs compared with the amount of swapping.

Transient routine   A supervisor routine that remains on the storage device with the remainder of the operating system.

Utility program   A program within an operating system that performs a specialized function.

Virtual memory   An extension of multiprogramming in which portions of programs not being used are kept in storage until needed, giving the impression that memory is unlimited; contrast with memory.

❑ SUMMARY

The set of step-by-step instructions to reach a solution to a problem is called a program. Two types of programs are system programs, which coordinate the operation of computer circuitry, and application programs, which solve particular user problems.

System programs are written for a particular type of computer and cannot be used on different machines without modification. A system programmer maintains the system programs and tailors them, if needed, to meet organizational requirements. System programs are normally provided by the computer manufacturer.

Application programs perform specific data-processing or computational tasks. An application programmer uses the capabilities of the computer for specific problems without needing an in-depth knowledge of the computer's circuitry.

An operating system is an integrated set of system programs that controls the functions of the CPU, input and output, and storage facilities. The operating system provides an interface between the user or application program and the computer hardware. The functions of an operating system are to eliminate human intervention, to allow several programs to share computer resources, to keep track of usage for fees, and to schedule jobs on a priority basis.

Two types of operating systems are batch and online. In a batch system, several user programs are grouped and processed one after the other. In an online system, the computer responds to spontaneous requests for resources. Operating systems currently in use do both. Operating system programs are kept online in a storage device called the system residence device. Two types of programs make up the operating system: control programs and processing programs.

Control programs include three programs. The supervisor program (monitor or executive), which coordinates the activities of all other parts of the operating system. Resident routines, the most frequently used components of the supervisor, are kept in memory; they may call transient routines from the storage device as needed. The job-control program, translates the job-control statements into machine language for the computer. These statements are written in a job-control language (JCL), which is the communication link between the programmer and the operating system. A job may be a single program or many related programs. The input/output management system, which oversees and coordinates input/output operations.

Processing programs assist users. They include language translators, linkage editors, library programs, and utility programs. Utility programs do specialized functions such as sorting and merging files. (The other programs are discussed in chapter 12.)

When the CPU is very active, the system is more efficient. Early computer systems used serial processing to execute programs—one at a time, one after another. Today, the CPU is used more efficiently through the use of multiprogramming, in which several programs are loaded into main memory and run concurrently. The programs are separated in memory by regions or partitions. The CPU works on different parts of different programs as resources are available. I/O devices handle resources as they are needed by the CPU. Each program is assigned a priority, but in large systems, this is not simple.

Sometimes programs do not fit into an assigned memory partition. Virtual memory uses paging or segmentation to give the illusion that an entire program is in memory. Programs are divided into pages or segments and are taken into memory as needed by the CPU through the action called swapping. In some programs, little actual processing occurs compared with the amount of processing. This is known as thrashing.

A CPU can only process one instruction at a time, but two or more CPUs can be linked together for coordinated operation in a technique known as multiprocessing. Instructions are executed simultaneously, but by different CPUs. One small CPU, called a front-end processor, can handle I/O interrupts, while the large CPU handles large mathematical calculations. When the small CPU is used as an interface between a large CPU and a large data base (rather than peripheral devices), it is termed a back-end processor. In many such configurations, the extra CPUs can be used as backup in case something happens to the primary CPU.

1. Two basic categories of programs are _____ programs.
    a. source and object
    c. system and application
    b. control and processing
    d. resident and transient

---

c. System programs coordinate the operation of computer circuitry, and application programs solve particular user problems.

2. System programs are normally written by _____.
    a. the computer manufacturer or a specialized programming firm
    b. the chief programming team
    c. a programmer analyst
    d. a team of programmers sent by the manufacturer to the purchaser of the computer

---

a. They are initially written in a general fashion to meet as many user requirements as possible. They can be modified to meet particular needs.

3. A difficulty with early computers was that _____.
    a. the operating systems contained many errors
    b. operating systems didn't even exist
    c. few people knew how to operate the operating systems
    d. the operators needed to know machine language

---

b. Human operators monitored computer operations, determined the way in which programs were run, and readied input and output devices.

4. The functions of an operating system are _____.
    a. determined by the user
    b. determined by the system programmer
    c. governed by the application programs
    d. geared toward attaining maximum efficiency

---

d. Functions include, among other things, eliminating human intervention, allowing programs to share computer resources, and setting job priorities.

5. Mainframe and minicomputer operating systems _____.
   a. give priority to online programs
   b. give priority to batch programs
   c. can handle batch and online simultaneously
   d. must finish batch programs before executing an online program

---

c. They respond to interrupts from I/O devices. Normal processing is suspended (the CPU is interrupted) so that the CPU may direct the operation of the I/O device.

6. Operating system programs are kept _____.
   a. in memory for immediate execution
   b. online in a storage device
   c. on tape
   d. in the input/output management system

---

b. The storage device is known as the system residence device. The media commonly used are magnetic tape and magnetic disk.

7. Resident routines are programs that _____.
   a. coordinate the activities of all other parts of the operating system
   b. reside in the system residence device and are called as needed
   c. remain in memory as long as the computer is running
   d. are also known collectively as the supervisor

---

c. Resident routines are the most frequently used components of the supervisor and are initially loaded into memory.

8. The communication link between the programmer and the operating system that helps instruct the operating system as to how a particular job is to be carried out is the _____.
   a. interrupt   c. utility program
   b. job-control language   d. input/output management system

---

b. The job-control language is typically used with the batch oriented portion of operating systems.

9. Multiprogramming _____.
    a. is a term that describes serial processing
    b. increases CPU active time
    c. is a synonym for multiprocessing
    d. enables multiple programs to be run simultaneously

---

b. Multiprogramming allocates computer resources and offsets low I/O speeds by having several programs in the memory unit at the same time.

10. Two or more CPUs linked together for coordinated operation is called _____.
    a. front-end processing   c. tandem processing
    b. multiprogramming   d. multiprocessing

---

d. Stored-program instructions are executed simultaneously, but by different CPUs.

❏ TRUE/FALSE

1. T F Interrupts originate with the operating system.

2. T F A single program is always called a job.

3. T F Pages are areas of fixed size in memory.

4. T F Sort/merge programs are a type of utility program.

5. T F Virtual memory offers tremendous flexibility to programmers and system analysts designing new applications.

6. T F A back-end processor is an interface between a large CPU and a large data base.

7. T F A limitation of multiprogramming is that each partition must be large enough to hold an entire program.

8. T F Virtual memory is the same as real memory.

9. T F A major problem of virtual memory is the need for extensive online storage.

10. T F A difficulty of multiprocessing is that if one CPU malfunctions, the whole system fails.

❏ MATCHING

a. control programs
b. real memory
c. front-end processor
d. supervisor program
e. segments

f. thrashing
g. operating system
h. serial processing
i. utility programs
j. swapping

1. The integrated set of system programs that controls the functions of the CPU, input and output, and storage facilities of the system is the _____.

2. The _____ coordinates the activities of all other parts of an operating system.

3. CPU memory is the same as _____.

4. Specialized functions such as sort/merge are done by _____.

5. Programs that oversee system operations and perform tasks such as input/output and scheduling are called _____.

6. Executing programs one at a time, one after another is called _____.

7. Variable-sized blocks called _____ hold logical parts of a program in some virtual memory systems.

8. Transferring a portion of a program from real memory to virtual memory and another portion from virtual to real is called _____.

9. The interface between a large CPU and peripheral devices is the _____.

10. _____ occurs when little actual processing occurs compared to the amount of pages or segments changed.

1. Explain the effect of interrupts.

2. What two types of programs make up an operating system?

3. What is the purpose of the job-control program?

4. Explain memory management or memory protection.

5. What is used to overcome the problem of limited physical space in multiprogramming?

6. What is the principle behind virtual memory?

7. Of what advantage is virtual memory to programmers and system analysts designing new applications?

8. How is segmentation different from paging?

9. Name two limitations of virtual memory.

10. Explain the difference between a front-end processor and a back-end processor.

CHAPTER 11

Software Development

❏ KEY TERMS

Branch A statement used to alter the normal flow of program execution.

Bug A program error.

Chief programmer team (CPT) A method of organization used in developing software systems in industry in which a chief programmer supervises the development and testing of software; programmer productivity and software reliability are increased.

Coding The process of writing a problem solution in a computer programming language.

Debugging The process of locating, isolating, and correcting errors within a program.

Desired output The portion of the software development process where the system's output is defined.

Desk checking A method used in both system and application program debugging in which the sequence of operations is mentally traced to verify the correctness of program logic.

Detail diagram A chart used in HIPO packages to describe the specific functions performed and data items used in a given module.

Flowchart Of two kinds: the program flowchart represents the types and sequences of operations in a program and the system flowchart shows the flow of data through a system.

Formal design review (structured walk-through) Also called a structured walk-through; an evaluation of the design of a software system by a group of managers, analysts, and programmers to determine completeness, accuracy, and quality of the design.

HIPO (Hierarchy plus Input-Process-Output) A method of diagramming a solution to a problem; highlights the inputs, processing, and outputs of program modules.

Informal design review An attempt to find problems early in the software development process.

Loop A structure that allows a specified sequence of instructions to be executed repeatedly as long as stated conditions remain true.

Modular approach   A method of simplifying a programming project by breaking it into segments or subunits referred to as modules.

Module   Part of a whole; a program segment or subsystem; a set of logically related program statements that perform one specified task in a program.

Needed input   The portion of the software development process where the input required to produce the desired output is determined.

Overview diagram   Used in HIPO packages to describe in greater detail a module shown in the visual table of contents.

Problem definition   The portion of the software development process where the problem to be solved is defined including desired output, needed input, and processing requirements.

Processing requirements   The portion of the software development process that turns needed input into desired output.

Program specifications   The documentation for a programming problem definition, it includes the desired output, the needed input, and the processing requirements.

Proper program   A structured program in which each individual segment or module has only one entrance and one exit.

Pseudocode   An informal design language used to represent the logic of a programming problem solution.

Reliability   The ability of a program to consistently obtain correct results.

Selection   A logic pattern that requires the computer to make a comparison; the result of the comparison determines which execution path will be taken next.

Simple sequence   A logic pattern in which one statement is executed after another, in the order in which they occur in the program.

Software development process   A sequence of four steps used to develop the solution to a programming problem in a structured manner. The steps are (1) define and document the problem, (2) design and document a solution, (3) write and document the program, and (4) debug and test the program and revise the documentation if necessary.

Structure chart   A graphic representation of the results of the top-down design process, displaying the modules of the solution and their relationships to one another; of two types, system and process.

Structured programming   A collection of techniques that encourages the development of well-designed, less error-prone programs with easy-to-follow logic. Structured programming techniques can be divided into two categories: (1) structured design techniques, such as top-down design, that are used in designing a problem solution, and (2) structured coding techniques, which state the rules that are followed when a program is actually coded.

Syntax   The grammatical rules of a language.

Testing   The process of executing a program with input data that is either a representative sample of actual data or a facsimile of it to determine if the program will always obtain correct results.

Top-down design   A method of defining a solution in terms of major functions to be performed, and further breaking down the major functions into subfunctions; the further the breakdown, the greater the detail.

Verification   Mathematical proof that a program or module is correctly designed.

Visual table of contents   Used in HIPO packages; includes blocks with identification numbers that are used as a reference in other HIPO diagrams.

❑ SUMMARY

The basic problem in programming is that the programmer must know how to instruct the computer in the exact steps it must take to solve a programming problem. The software development process is used to develop a solution to a programming problem. The steps in the software development process are as follows: 1) define and document the problem, 2) design and document a solution, 3) write and document the program, and 4) debug and test the program and revise the documentation.

A person called a system analyst is often used to define and design a solution to a programming problem. In the software development process, the documentation of the problem should include a description of the desired output, needed input, and processing requirements. This documentation is referred to as the program specifications.

When designing a tentative solution, it is not necessary to know what programming language will be used. All languages use four basic logic patterns or variations thereof: simple sequence, selection, loop, and branch. The simple sequence executes one statement after another in the program order. The selection pattern (or conditional programming logic) requires the computer to make a choice based on the results of a comparison (e.g., greater than, equal to, or less than). The loop enables a computer to repeat one or more instructions as many times as needed. The branch pattern allows the computer to skip statements in the program, leaving them unexecuted. The branch pattern is considered poor programming practice.

In the early days of software development, programming was an art. No rules were followed, and thus, productivity was low. Programs were unreliable, failed with invalid data, and were hard to maintain in working order. These problems led to studies of programming techniques. Two mathematicians, Jacopini and Bohm, discovered that the branch pattern was unnecessary, and in 1968, Dijkstra wrote a paper criticizing the GOTO statement. Soon computer scientists were writing languages that did not use the branch. They also structured programs by breaking them into manageable modules, or subprograms, each designed to do a specific task. These techniques are referred to as structured programming, in which program logic is readily apparent and fewer programming errors result.

Designing a program should proceed from the general to the specific in top-down design. Top-down design uses the modular approach, breaking a problem into smaller and smaller subproblems, and is sometimes called the "divide and conquer" method. Using top-down design helps discover errors early and bring a problem down to manageable size. Top-down design is illustrated with structure charts and Hierarchy plus Input-Process-Output (HIPO) packages.

After the program structure is complete, logic is written in pseudocode, a narrative description of program logic that includes key words such as PRINT, IF/THEN/ELSE, END, and READ. Flowcharts are used to graphically show program logic. They are designed to flow top-to-bottom and left-to-right. Action diagrams also show the designed solution to a problem in a top-down fashion, and eliminate the need to mix the different types of charts and drawings.

Other techniques for developing software include the Chief Programmer Team (CPT) and the structured walk-through. A CPT consists of one or more programmers and a librarian under the supervision of a chief programmer. A walk-through involves allowing a formal review team to check a program before actual coding takes place.

The third step in program design is writing and documenting the program. The program is written in a specific programming language; this process is called coding. To code a program, the syntax, or grammatical rules, of the language must be followed. Rules for structured coding limit the use of GOTO statements, regulate the size of program modules, define a proper program, and require thorough documentation. (A proper program has only one entrance and exit per module with modules limited to 50 to 60 lines.) Programming statements common to most high-level programming languages are comments, declarations, input/output statements, computations, comparisons, and loops.

The last step in program design is debugging and testing the program. Errors in a program are called bugs. Error correction is called debugging. Numerous techniques have been developed to aid in debugging. The language translator locates syntax errors. Next, the program is tested by executing the program with input data that is a sample of actual data or a facsimile of the data. Desk checking, a testing technique, involves having the programmer pretend to be the computer. Dumps list the contents of registers and memory locations, and trace programs list the steps followed during processing in the order in which they occurred. A newer technique called verification involves the process of mathematically proving the correctness of a program through the use of predicate calculus.

1. The basic problem in programming is that the programmer must know _____.
   a. exactly how a computer works
   b. how to instruct the computer to solve a problem
   c. everything about the user's business
   d. the operating system as well as the programming language to be used

---

b. People often solve problems intuitively. Computers lack this capability. The programmer must instruct the computer in the exact steps in an ordered way.

2. The four basic logic patterns for a computer are _____.
   a. simple sequence, selection, loop, and branch
   b. sequence, print, read, and loop
   c. branch, sequence, GOTO, and compare
   d. add, subtract, multiply, and divide

---

a. Programming languages may have more complicated statements, but they are all based on various combinations of these four patterns.

3. Documentation for needed input, desired output, and processing steps is referred to as the _____.
   a. problem definition   c. software development process
   b. program specifications   d. program logic

---

b. The documentation describes the problem definition, but is called the program specifications.

4. The logic pattern that is not recommended for use by the proponents of structured programming techniques is the _____ pattern.
   a. simple sequence   c. selection
   b. loop   d. branch

---

d. The branch, or GOTO, pattern often contributes to convoluted logic and "spaghetti" programming that is hard to follow and hard to debug.

5. In program design, proceeding from the general to the specific is known as _____.
    a. structured programming
    b. top-down design
    c. proper programming
    d. conditional programming

b. Top-down design employs the modular approach, which consists of breaking a problem into smaller and smaller subproblems. The major steps or functions are defined first.

---

6. A narrative, English-like description of the logic of a program is called _____.
    a. pseudocode
    b. a structure chart
    c. a HIPO package
    d. an overview diagram

---

a. Pseudocode allows the programmer to focus on the steps required to perform a particular process, rather than on the syntax of a language.

7. Without standards and structure, early software development _____.
    a. often resulted in spending more for software than for hardware
    b. often produced unreliable programs
    c. was based on modular programming
    d. was an art, and resulted in high programmer productivity

---

b. With no structure or guidelines for program design and testing, programmers often wrote software that produced incorrect results.

8. An important goal of programming is to _____.
    a. get the program coded as soon as possible
    b. produce an error-free program in the shortest possible time
    c. avoid errors regardless of the time involved
    d. employ all four basic logic patterns

---

b. Meeting this goal requires the early detection of errors in order to prevent expensive and time-consuming modifications later.

9. When the programmer pretends to be the computer to locate program errors, this is called _____.
    a. structured walkthrough
    b. desk checking
    c. informal design review
    d. verification

---

b. The programmer attempts to find flaws in logic by reading each instruction and simulating how the computer would process a data item.

10. One aid used to debug and test a program lists the steps followed during program execution in the order in which they occurred and is called _____.
  a. desk checking
  b. a trace
  c. a dump
  d. a structured walkthrough

---

b. A trace actually lists these steps in order. Desk checking only attempts to do this.

❏ TRUE/FALSE

1. T F Flowchart symbols are arranged from general to specific.

2. T F It is not necessary to know what programming language will be used in order to develop the logic of a solution.

3. T F The branch logic pattern is extremely versatile and its use is recommended whenever possible.

4. T F Jacopini and Bohm discovered that the selection logic pattern was unnecessary.

5. T F Top-down design is referred to as the "divide and conquer" method.

6. T F The lowest-level modules of a structure chart contain the most general level of organization.

7. T F A disadvantage of flowcharts is that they take many pages and are confusing as the program becomes more complex.

8. T F A program module should be limited to 50 to 60 lines.

9. T F A program segment is a proper program when it has one entrance and one exit.

10. T F If a program is modified, its documentation must also be modified.

❑ MATCHING

a. modules
b. verification
c. structure chart
d. program specifications
e. flowchart

f. syntax
g. selection
h. HIPO
i. debugging
j. declaration

1. The documentation for the input, output, and processing steps are the _____.

2. The _____ logic pattern requires that the computer make a choice.

3. A statement that defines items used in a program is the _____ statement.

4. Manageable subprograms designed to do a specific task are called _____.

5. A _____ graphically illustrates the various modules and their relationship to one another.

6. _____ packages are visual aids that highlight the input, processing, and output of program modules.

7. The actual flow of logic of a program can be found in a _____.

8. The grammatical rules of a particular programming language are known as _____.

9. The process of locating, isolating, and eliminating errors is called _____.

10. The process of mathematically proving the correctness of a program is called _____.

❑ SHORT ANSWER

1. List the four steps in the software development process.

2. Explain the loop logic pattern.

3. List some problems of early haphazard programming.

4. What is the advantage of using action diagrams for documenting the design of the solution to a problem?

5. What are the two broad categories structured programming techniques?

6. Name some advantages of top-down design.

7. Explain the difference between the informal and formal design review.

8. Why do corporations use system analysts rather than programmers to define and design a solution to a programming problem?

9. List some programming statements common to most high-level languages.

10. What is a dump? Compare its use to a trace.

CHAPTER 12

Programming Languages

❏ KEY TERMS

Ada A high-level programming language developed for use by the Department of Defense; named for Augusta Ada Byron, Countess of Lovelace and daughter of the poet Lord Byron; Ada is a sophisticated structured language that supports concurrent processing.

Assembler program The translator program for an assembly language program; produces a machine-language program (object program) that can then be executed.

Assembly language A low-level, symbolic programming language that uses convenient abbreviations called mnemonics rather than groupings of 0s and 1s used in machine language. Because instructions in assembly language generally have a one-to-one correspondence with machine-language instructions, assembly language is easier to translate into machine language than are high-level language statements.

BASIC (Beginners' All-purpose Symbolic Instruction Code) A high-level programming language commonly used for interactive problem solving by users; it is widely implemented on microcomputers and is often taught to beginning programmers.

C A high-level programming language that includes low-level language instructions; C is popular because it is portable and is implemented on a wide variety of computer systems.

COBOL (COmmon Business-Oriented Language) A high-level programming language generally used for business applications; it is well suited to manipulating large data files.

Compiler program The translator program for a high-level language such as FORTRAN or COBOL; translates the entire source program into machine language, creating an object program that can be executed.

FORTRAN (FORmula TRANslator) The oldest high-level programming language; used primarily in performing mathematical or scientific operations.

General-purpose language A computer programming language used to solve a wide variety of programming problems.

High-level language A computer programming language that is oriented toward the human programmer rather than the computer itself.

Input/output-bound A situation in which the CPU is slowed down because of I/O operations, which are extremely slow in comparison to CPU internal processing speeds.

Interpreter program A high-level language translator that evaluates and translates a program one statement at a time; used extensively on microcomputer systems because it takes less memory than a compiler.

Label A name written beside a programming instruction that acts as an identifier for that instruction.

Librarian program Software that manages the storage and use of library programs by maintaining a directory of programs in the system library and appropriate procedures for additions and deletions.

Linkage editor A subprogram of the operating system that links the object program from the system residence device to application program object modules.

Logo An education-oriented, procedure-oriented interactive programming language designed to allow anyone to begin programming and communicating with computers quickly.

Low-level language A computer programming language that is oriented toward the computer rather than toward a programmer.

Machine language The only set of instructions that a computer can execute directly; a code that designates the proper electrical states in the computer as combinations of 0s and 1s.

Mnemonics Symbolic names or memory aids used in symbolic languages (for example, assembly language) and high-level programming languages.

Natural language A language, designed primarily for novice computer users, that uses English-like statements, usually for the purpose of accessing data in a data base.

Object program A sequence of machine executable instructions derived from source-program statements by a language-translator program.

Op code (operation code) The part of a machine or assembly language instruction that tells the computer what function to perform.

Operand The part of an instruction that tells the computer where to find the data or equipment on which to operate.

Pascal A high-level structured programming language that was originally developed for instructional purposes and that is now commonly used in a wide variety of applications.

Portable Characteristic of a program that can be run on many different computers with minimal changes.

Problem-oriented language A programming language with which the problem and solution can be described without requiring a high level of programming skill.

Procedure-oriented language A programming language with the emphasis placed on the computational and logical procedures required to solve a problem.

Process-bound A condition that occurs when a program monopolizes the processing facilities of the computer, making it impossible for other programs to be executed.

Special-purpose language A programming language designed for a specific use.

Structured language A computer programming language that is used to develop programs that are modular, logical, and easy to modify and maintain.

System library A collection of files in which various parts of an operating system are stored.

Unstructured language A computer programming language that results in programs that are poorly organized and difficult to modify and maintain.

❑ SUMMARY

Programming languages are communication systems that people use to communicate with computers. Early computers used machine and assembly languages, which were tedious and dependent on the type of computer being used. FORTRAN began the trend toward high-level languages. Today, there are more than 200 distinct programming languages.

High-level languages have the potential to be portable (executable on a variety of systems) when written according to the American National Standards Institute (ANSI). Many manufacturers do not follow standards and add extra features or enhancements.

Languages can be categorized different ways: low-level or high-level; structured or unstructured; procedure-oriented or problem-oriented; and general purpose or special purpose. Many languages fall somewhere in between the extremes of these categories.

Before programs written in languages other than machine language can be executed, they must be translated into machine language. Assembly-language programs are translated by an assembler program. High-level language programs are translated by compilers or interpreters. Compilers translate the entire source program into machine code, or an object program, which is "linked" with other object programs. These object programs are referred to as the load module, which is executed by the CPU. Interpreters translate the source program one statement at a time.

Low-level languages are oriented towards the hardware. Machine language is the only language that the computer is able to execute directly. It is often coded in either octal (base 8) or hexadecimal (base 16) codes. Machine language allows the computer to execute commands efficiently and allows the programmer to fully utilize the computer's potential. It is error prone and rarely used today. Each machine language instruction has two parts: the op code and the operand.

Assembly language uses mnemonics (symbolic names) to specify machine operations. It is often used for writing operating systems. Three parts of an assembly language instruction are op code, operand, and label.

High-level languages are oriented toward the user. Meaningful words are compiled or translated into machine code for execution. FORTRAN (FORmula TRANslator) is the oldest high-level language dating back to the mid-1950s. It has excellent mathematical capabilities.

BASIC (Beginner's All-purpose Symbolic Instruction Code) is a simplified version of FORTRAN intended to teach programming to students. It is a general-purpose language and popular for use with microcomputers.

Pascal was the first major language to implement the ideas and methodology of structured programming. Named for Blaise Pascal, it is an easy-to-learn general-purpose language, has graphic capabilities, and uses modules that can be nested. Pascal is being adapted inexpensively for use with microcomputers.

COBOL (COmmon Business Oriented Language) is the most frequently used business language. The Department of Defense helped form CODASYL (Conference On DAta SYstem Languages) to write COBOL. COBOL uses many English words and is self-documenting. It is easy to maintain and has strong file-handling capabilities.

Ada is a state-of-the-art language derived from Pascal and designed for the Department of Defense. It is named for Augusta Ada Byron, who worked with Charles Babbage. Ada is a difficult language for beginners to learn. It has concurrent processing capabilities.

C is a structured, middle-level language used for both system and application programs. C was used to write the UNIX operating system. It is a portable, general-purpose language that can be used on systems ranging from microcomputers to supercomputers.

Logo is a structured, procedure-oriented, interactive language designed as a teaching tool for children. Logo uses graphics and a "turtle" to teach logic and programming.

Very high-level languages, or fourth-generation languages, require adherence to a programming syntax but are much easier to use than high-level languages. They include three tools for program development: query languages, report generators, and application generators.

Natural or query languages are languages that attempt to allow the user to state queries in English-like sentences. They are primarily for the inexperienced computer user for data bases.

Choosing a language to use depends on several factors. For example, business applications tend to be input/output bound. Scientific applications tend to be process-bound. Two or more languages can be used by a firm to solve different problems.

❏ STRUCTURED LEARNING

1. The lowest-level language is called _____.
   a. BASIC
   b. machine language
   c. assembly language
   d. FORTRAN

---

b. Codes called machine language correspond to the on/off electrical states in a computer.

2. The most influential agency in computer language standards is _____.
   a. ANSI
   b. ASCII
   c. CODASYL
   d. MIT

---

a. American National Standards Institute has developed or adopted widely used standards for many languages, although many manufacturers do not entirely adhere to these standards.

3. The parts of an assembly language instruction are _____.
   a. mnemonics and op codes
   b. op code, operand, label
   c. binary, hexadecimal, octal
   d. mnemonics and assembler

---

b. The op code tells the computer what function to perform. The operand tells what data to use. The label is a name that represents the location of a particular instruction.

4. A programming language in which the problem and solution are described without the necessary procedures being specified is a(n) _____ language.
   a. general-purpose
   b. unstructured
   c. high-level
   d. problem-oriented

---

d. Problem-oriented languages require little programming skill.

5. Among BASIC's most attractive features is its _____.
   a. portability and structure
   b. simplicity and flexibility
   c. graphics and file-handling capabilities
   d. problem-oriented focus

---

b. BASIC can be used for solving a wide variety of problems and is easy to learn by novice programmers.

6. Pascal is well known and has achieved widespread use because _____.
   a. it was named after Blaise Pascal
   b. it is easy to learn
   c. it has an ANSI standard
   d. it is a highly structured language

---

d. Pascal is popular because it helps students learn good programming habits using the structured features offered by Pascal. It was the first programming language to implement the ideas and methods of structured programming.

7. Natural languages have been designed primarily for _____.
   a. the novice user for online data base
   b. teaching children to program
   c. microcomputer users
   d. structured programming uses

---

a. Natural language processors are used with a vocabulary of words and definitions that allows the processor to translate the English-like sentences to machine executable form.

8. Interpreter programs can be inefficient because _____.
   a. they are written in machine language
   b. they need a lot of memory to store an object program
   c. they require storage space for the interpreter program
   d. a statement used more than once in a program must be evaluated, translated, and executed each time it is used.

---

d. An interpreter evaluates and translates a program one statement at a time. It translates the statement into machine language and executes it before proceeding to the next statement.

9. The program that is translated from assembly or high-level language into machine language for processing is called the _____ before it is translated.
   a. source program   c. compiler
   b. object program   d. interpreter

___

a. The source program is the sequence of instructions written by the programmer. It must be translated into machine language for processing.

10. Primary uses of the language C are _____.
   a. system programming, utility programs, and graphics applications
   b. graphics applications and file handling
   c. instructional uses and structured programming
   d. business functions

___

a. C has some capabilities similar to those of assembly language such as manipulating individual bits and bytes. One well-known C project is the UNIX operating system.

❏ TRUE/FALSE

1. T F   A compiler translates a source program into a machine-language object program.

2. T F   An advantage of machine and assembly languages is that they are machine dependent.

3. T F   A machine-language program is always written in binary form.

4. T F   Logo has few uses other than teaching good programming habits to children.

5. T F   BASIC is a highly standardized language.

6. T F   COBOL supports sequential, indexed, and direct access files.

7. T F   FORTRAN is the oldest high-level language.

8. T F   Different languages cannot be combined in the same program.

9. T F   The trend in programming is away from using assembly languages.

10. T F   The translator for assembly language is called an assembler program.

❑ MATCHING

a. query   f. Logo
b. interpreter   g. input-output
c. portable   h. machine dependent
d. process   i. compiler
e. mnemonics   j. Ada

1.   When a language is able to be executed on a wide variety of systems with minimal changes, it is described as _____.

2.   A sophisticated and reliable language that supports multiprogramming is _____.

3.   An apt description of machine language is _____.

4.   Assembly language uses symbolic names called _____.

5.   The language simple enough for children to learn yet powerful enough to be used in teaching geometry and physics is _____.

6.   Another name for a natural language is a(n) _____ language.

7.   Many business application languages are _____ bound.

8.   Scientific programming tends to be _____ bound.

9.   The program that produces a machine-language object program from the source program a programmer writes is a(n) _____.

10. The language-translator program that evaluates and translates a program one statement at a time is a(n) _____.

❑ SHORT ANSWER

1. What is the difference between low-level and high-level languages?

2. What is meant by a structured language?

3. What is the difference between a procedure-oriented and a problem-oriented language?

4. What is the difference between a general-purpose and a special-purpose language?

5. Name an advantage of an assembly language.

6. Name two questions that a company should ask when deciding what programming language to use for a particular application.

7. What does the acronym BASIC stand for? COBOL?

8. Explain the three tools contained in very high-level programming languages.

9. What is unique about the way the programming language Logo encourages programming skills?

10. By whom and under what circumstances what the programming language Ada developed?

CHAPTER 13

Application Software

❑ KEY TERMS

Cell   The unique location in an electronic spreadsheet where a row and column intersect.

Data-base management system (DBMS)   A set of programs that serves as the interface between the data base and the programmer, operating system, and users; also programs used to design and maintain data bases.

Data definition language (DDL)   The language in which the schema, which states how records within a data base are related, is written. This language differs depending on the type of data-base management system being used.

Data manipulation language (DML)   The language used to access a hierarchical or a network data base to provide a way for users to access the data base. The data manipulation language is different for each type of data-base management system.

Decision support system (DSS)   An integrated system that draws on data from a wide variety of sources such as data bases to provide a supportive tool for managerial decision-making. Generally, managers use fourth-generation programming languages to access decision support systems.

Electronic spreadsheet   An electronic ledger sheet used to store and manipulate any type of numerical data.

End-user development tools (fourth-generation software development tools)   Tools that allow the end-user to develop an application package, usually through the use of a fourth-generation programming language. Examples of end-user development tools include simulation software, statistical packages, and data-base management systems.

Expert system   Form of artificial intelligence software designed to imitate the same decision-making and evaluation processes of experts in a specific field.

File manager   An application package designed to duplicate the traditional manual methods of filing records.

Functional tools   A category of application software packages that perform specific tasks or functions, such as inventory control.

Graphics package An application software package designed to allow the user to display images on the display screen or printer.

Productivity tools Application software packages that can increase the productivity of the user. Examples are text processors and graphic packages.

Schema A program that describes how records and files within a data base are related to one another.

Simulation The use of a model to project the outcome of a particular real-world situation.

Spelling checker Application software that checks words in a document against a dictionary file. Any words in the document that are not in the file are flagged; often included in word processing packages.

Statistical package A software package that performs statistical analysis of data. Examples are SAS, SPSS, and Minitab.

Turnkey system An integrated system including hardware, software, training, and support developed for particular businesses.

Word processor An application software package designed for the preparation of text; enables the user to do writing, editing, formatting, and printing functions.

❏ SUMMARY

The court decision forcing IBM to "unbundle" its software led to the growth of the software industry, and businesses soon realized the advantages of buying commercial software. Using commercial software was cheaper than developing it in house. Commercial packages contained more features because of their quality and sophistication, they were reliable, and the vendor provided support and training. They did not, however, always meet the user's exact needs and the vendor did not always provide total support.

There are three broad categories of application software: productivity tools, functional tools, and end-user development tools.

Productivity tools are packages that can increase user productivity. Examples are word processors, graphics packages, electronic spreadsheets, file managers, desktop organizers, text outliners, integrated software, and keyboard macro packages. They are aids in achieving a goal. Word processors enable the user to manipulate documents consisting of text, such as reports and tables. They may include extensions such as spelling checkers and mail-merge capabilities. Graphics packages enable the user to create bar graphs, line graphs, and pie charts. The results are sometimes called presentation graphics. An electronic spreadsheet is a computerized version of a traditional spreadsheet, or ledger sheet. Labels, values, and formulas are entered into cells, the points on a spreadsheet where rows and columns intersect. Formulas can be applied to the contents of cells to obtain results, the application of which is useful in "what-if" analysis. File managers duplicate traditional manual methods of filing. They keep records necessary for a particular business department.

Functional tools are packages for doing specific functions in accounting, manufacturing, sales, marketing, and desktop publishing. (Desktop publishing software allows users to create near-typeset quality documents by using a laser printer in conjunction with their computer system.) Many functional packages consist of modules. The user purchases the modules needed and can add others later. The modules interact with one another, passing data between them.

Different types of functional tools include Manufacturing Resource Planning (MRP) packages (used for business planning, production planning, and scheduling) and computer-aided design (CAD), computer-aided engineering (CAE), and computer-aided manufacturing (CAM) software (used for designing products, testing the designs, and controlling the manufacturing). Computer-Aided Systems Engineering (CASE) packages automate the step-by-step process of developing software by capturing the information required for each step from the user. Sales analysis software is used to analyze data on sales transactions over a given period of time. It is used in ordering and maintaining order records.

Tools designed for the horizontal market are for general use and are not customized. Tools designed for the vertical market are very specific and can be tailored. They are designed for the particular user and all support is provided. These are termed turnkey systems.

End-user development tools, or fourth-generation software development tools, are packages with which the end-user can develop a software application for the specific needs of the situation. They include simulation software, decision support systems, and expert systems. These tools use fourth-generation programming languages, or query languages, which require little skill. The user must learn the commands and syntax, however.

Simulation software enables the creation of a model to project what will happen in a particular situation. Simulation is useful in making business decisions.

Decision Support Systems (DSS) help managers to make and implement decisions. They are fully integrated, obtaining data from a wide variety of sources. They enable users to analyze data on an interactive basis. DSSs use fourth-generation languages to query data bases for necessary information. They include spreadsheets and statistical analysis, and also have graphics and report-generating features.

Expert systems mimic the decision-making processes of human experts in narrowly defined fields. Expert systems are different from DSS because they cover very small fields of knowledge. DSS enable managers to make decisions based on a wide range of data and factors. Expert systems are unable to make the inferences that humans can. Expert systems are used for diagnosing diseases, plan estates, and locate mineral deposits.

Statistical packages can perform elaborate procedures accurately and quickly. Functions include calculating means, ranges, variances, and deviations.

Data-base management systems (DBMS) are a series of programs that are used to design and maintain data bases. Three categories are hierarchical, network, and relational. Hierarchical and network systems use programs called schemas written in data definition language (DDL). A data manipulation language (DML) allows users to access the data base. A relational data base uses a fourth-generation language such as SQL (Structured Query Language).

In choosing an application software package, many questions need to be answered. The user should consider four areas: performance, operations, I/O functionality, and vendor support. Perhaps the best way is to try a number of packages on a trial basis to determine how each will actually perform on the job.

❏ STRUCTURED LEARNING

1. Because of the reliability and features of commercial application software, _____.
   a. IBM had to unbundle its software
   b. many companies discontinued much of their in-house software development
   c. professional computer scientists began to categorize the packages
   d. the software needed a great deal of modification to suit a company's particular needs

---

b. The cost of in-house development became prohibitive compared to the costs, versatility, and number of features found in commercial packages.

2. Word processors are used for _____.
   a. manipulating documents consisting of text, such as reports and tables
   b. creating bar graphs, line graphics, and pie charts
   c. creating slides from images on terminal screens
   d. duplicating the manual methods of filing

---

a. Text can be deleted, inserted, or moved; margins can be set and footnotes inserted.

3. Spreadsheets are useful for calculating interest rates because _____.
   a. they are specifically designed for calculating interest
   b. they were designed by a former banker
   c. formulas can be applied to the contents of cells to get a result
   d. they contain accounting modules

---

c. The ability to alter variables within the spreadsheet makes such calculations a simple matter.)

4. Packages with built-in modules _____.
   a. are difficult to tailor to the user
   b. enable the user to add modules as needed
   c. cannot pass data between them
   d. need a different user per module

---

b. When a company purchases a particular package, only those modules needed are obtained. Others can be added later to tailor the package to individual needs.

5. A functional tool for the horizontal market _____.
   a. is designed for general use
   b. can easily be tailored
   c. is known as a turnkey system
   d. is a productivity tool

---

a. A tool for the horizontal market is designed for general use and could not be customized for a particular business.

6. Desktop publishing packages enable users to use graphics features in designing documents and

_____.
   a. are facilitated by the WYSIWYG feature
   b. are classified as end-user development tools
   c. are examples of simulation software
   d. are productivity tools

---

a. WYSIWYG—what you see is what you get—enables the user to see what a document will look like without making a large number of printouts.

7. Decision support systems _____.
   a. are programs written by a software company
   b. contain a variety of tools such as fourth-generation languages, electronic spreadsheets, statistical analysis, and graphics
   c. are used with the Pascal programming language
   d. are the same as expert systems

---

b. They allow the user to analyze data on an interactive basis. They can be used to simulate specified conditions to determine the output of a particular situation.

8. Expert systems have the advantage that _____.
   a. they can make the same inferences that a human can
   b. enable the user to query using any language
   c. cover a wide variety of data and factors
   d. knowledge is not lost as it may be when a human dies

---

d. Software designers try to program the computer to follow the same path of thinking as top experts in the field do.

9. The fourth-generation language approved by ANSI is _____.
   a. SQL   c. C
   b. DDL   d. BASIC

---

a. Structured Query Language is used to query relational data bases. It does not require the skill of a data manipulation language.

10. One source of information on a commercial package is _____.
   a. schemas   c. ANSI
   b. user surveys   d. CODASYL

---

b. The DATAMATION publication conducts a yearly survey of data processing managers, asking them to evaluate packages they are using.

❑ TRUE/FALSE

1. T F Software vendors often provide "hot-line" phone numbers to assist users.

2. T F In the early days of commercial packages, providing support was often a problem.

3. T F Spelling checkers allow users to add words to the dictionary.

4. T F Each cell in a spreadsheet is a unique location.

5. T F A spreadsheet can only handle numbers, not letters.

6. T F Manufacturing resource planning packages help to keep overhead at a minimum.

7. T F A turnkey system is a complete system, like a car, with which all the user needs to do is turn it on.

8. T F Query languages are easy for nonprogrammers, but the user needs to learn the commands and syntax.

9. T F If a simulation works correctly, it can then be used to build a model.

10. T F A relational data base employs programs called schemas.

❑ MATCHING

a. expert systems
b. fourth-generation
c. word
d. data manipulation language
e. simulation

f. vertical
g. decision support systems
h. electronic spreadsheet
i. DBMS
j. functional tools

1. Programs that enable the user to manipulate documents consisting of text, such as reports and letters, are called _____ processors.

2. A computerized version of a traditional ledger sheet is the _____.

3. Accounting, manufacturing, sales, and marketing packages are examples of _____.

4. Turnkey systems are designed for the _____ market.

5. Using a model to project what will happen in a particular situation is called _____.

6. _____ software development tools are packages with which the end-user can develop a package addressing the particular needs of a situation.

7. An information system that helps managers make and implement decisions is called a(n) _____.

8. Programs that mimic the decision-making processes of human experts in narrowly defined fields are called _____.

9. A set of programs used to design and maintain a data base is called a(n) _____.

10. A program written in a(n) _____ determines how users can access a data base.

1. Name three advantages of commercial software.

2. What are the three broad categories of commercial software packages?

3. Name four examples of productivity tools.

4. What package is often used to prepare presentations, especially in business?

5. Name three examples of functional tools.

6. Describe the difference between tools for horizontal and vertical markets.

7. What is the advantage of a simulation package?

8. Name some specific uses of expert systems.

9. How are expert systems different from decision support systems?

10. What four areas does DATAMATION consider in evaluating software packages?

 **CHAPTER 14**

System Analysis and Design

❏ KEY TERMS

Action entry   One of four sections of a decision logic table; tells what actions should be taken.

Action stub   One of four sections of a decision logic table; describes possible actions applicable to the decision being made.

Condition entry   One of four sections of a decision logic table; answers questions in the condition stub.

Condition stub   One of four sections of a decision logic table; describes all options to be considered in making a decision.

Decision logic table (DLT)   A table that organizes relevant facts in a clear and concise manner to aid a decision-making process.

Direct (crash) conversion   A method of system implementation in which the old system is completely abandoned and the new one implemented all at once.

Edit check   A processing statement designed to identify potential errors in the input data.

Grid chart (tabular chart)   A chart used in system analysis and design to summarize the relationships between the functions of an organization.

Menu-driven system design   An application program is said to be menu-driven when it provides the user with "menus" displaying available choices or selections to help guide the user through the process of using the software.

Online storage   Storage that is in direct communication with the computer.

Parallel conversion   A system implementation approach in which the new system is operated side by side with the old one until all differences are reconciled and problems worked out.

Phased conversion   A method of system implementation in which the new system is implemented one portion at a time throughout the organization.

Pilot conversion   An approach to system implementation in which the new system is implemented in only one part of the organization at a time.

System analysis   The process of determining the requirements for implementing and maintaining an information system.

System analysis report   A report given to top management after the system analysis phase has been completed to report the findings of the system study; includes a statement of objectives, constraints, and possible alternatives.

System design report   The phase of a system life cycle in which the information system design alternatives are developed and presented to management. These alternatives should contain information on system inputs, processing, and outputs.

System flowchart   The group of symbols that represents the general information flow; focuses on inputs and outputs rather than on internal computer operations.

User-friendly   An easy-to-use, understandable software design that makes it easy for noncomputer personnel to use an application software package.

❑ SUMMARY

System analysis involves determining the requirements for designing, implementing, and maintaining an information system. The analyst must form a statement of business objectives_the goals of the system and acquire a general understanding of the scope of the analysis.

Reviewing the system from top down helps the analyst determine on what level the analysis should be conducted. The analyst then prepares a proposal that gives a clear reason for system analysis, defines the level of analysis, identifies the information needed to conduct the analysis, and sets up a schedule for analysis.

Reasons for conducting system analysis include the following: Information systems do not always function properly and require adjustment; new requirements, such as government regulations, require a new system analysis; new data-processing technology may be introduced; and an increase in sales or competition can cause an organization to make broad improvements.

The data required for system analysis is collected from internal sources of data (including personal interviews, system flowcharts, questionnaires, and formal reports) and external sources of data (such as books, periodicals, customers, and information from other companies). Data collection focuses on what is being done.

Data must be organized and analyzed to determine why certain operations and procedures are used. Several techniques are available. A tabular or grid chart is used to summarize relationships among components of a system. System flowcharts show the general flow of data through the system and include symbols that indicate actual media. A decision logic table (DLT) is a tabular representation of the actions to be taken under various conditions. Condition stubs and action stubs indicate condition and action entries. The condition entry points to the action to be taken.

After collecting and analyzing data, a system analysis report is made to management for the project's approval or termination. The report should include a restatement of scope and objectives, an explanation of the present system, a list of constraints and alternatives, a preliminary report of possible alternatives, and an estimate of resources and capital required.

If the system analysis report is approved by management, the system design phase begins. The design phase concentrates on how a system can be developed to meet information requirements. The steps include the following:

- Goals and objectives are reviewed.
- A system model is developed through flowcharts or diagrams.
- Organizational constraints such as budgets, time, and human factors are evaluated.
- Feasible alternative designs are developed with at least one design being manual.
- A feasibility analysis is done to ensure that all options are possible with the given constraints.
- A cost-benefit analysis is done to gain the greatest return on the tangible and intangibl benefits.
- A system design report is prepared for management. The report explains how the various designs will satisfy the requirements and makes a recommendation. Management approves the recommendation, makes changes, or selects none of the alternatives.

System programming involves writing the necessary programs. Programs should be divided into modules, each fully tested, and the entire program tested. The whole system must be documented in three areas: system documentation, program documentation, and procedure documentation. In designing solutions to business problems, analysts and programmers must also be aware of special considerations. Some of these issues are how the program should ask for data, what processing steps are needed to verify the accuracy of data and identify potential errors, and whether soft-copy output is needed.

System implementation converts ideas and flowcharts into reality. Personnel must be trained through seminars, tutorial sessions, and on-the-job training. Conversion to the new system completes the implementation. Parallel conversion runs the old and new systems side-by-side until the new is proven. Pilot conversion converts a small portion of the system over the entire organization to test it. Phased conversion replaces old segments with new—one at a time—throughout the organization. Crash (direct) conversion converts the entire system at once.

Then the system is audited and reviewed. Feedback from the user helps to determine if modification is necessary. All systems must be maintained to detect and correct errors, meet new needs, and respond to changes. A well designed information system is flexible and adaptable. Minor changes are normally necessary, and major changes become necessary over time.

In the traditional method of system design and analysis, the system design phase involves developing a system model. Prototyping can be used instead. It develops a working model of the system that is used during the design stage. The purpose is to solicit feedback from the end-user before the final design stage. Using prototyping should result in a system that more closely meets the needs of the user.

❏ STRUCTURED LEARNING

1. The system analysis report is for _____.
   - a. the analyst
   - b. the programmer
   - c. the workers
   - d. management

---

d. On the basis of this report, management decides whether to continue with the project.

2. One reason for conducting a system analysis is _____.
   - a. to gather the results of interviews
   - b. to do the cost/benefit analysis
   - c. that current reports provide incorrect information
   - d. to prepare a system analysis proposal

---

c. Conducting a system analysis may be necessary because the current system does not function properly.

3. The type and amount of data gathered for the system analysis report depends on _____.
   - a. internal and external sources
   - b. interview
   - c. the scope and goals of the system analysis
   - d. the top-down view of the organization's information system

---

c. Data can be supplied by internal and external sources depending on the scope and goals of the system analysis.

4. Creating and maintaining an effective data base requires that _____.
   - a. the data base have only one program
   - b. data items must be independent
   - c. all data is contained in one file
   - d. file processing be used

b. Data must be analyzed and organized from a corporate-wide perspective. The goal is to properly relate each data item to all other data items, ignoring departmental boundaries.

5. The first step in constructing a decision logic table is to _____.
   a. determine what conditions must be considered
   b. make the condition entries
   c. determine what actions can take place
   d. record the facts collected during the investigation of the old system

---

a. Decision logic tables summarize the logic required to make a decision in a form that is easy to understand.

6. The system design step that represents symbolically the system's major components in order to verify understanding of the components and their interaction is known as _____.
   a. developing alternative designs   c. performing cost/benefit analysis
   b. performing feasibility analysis   d. developing a system model

---

d. The analyst may use flowcharts to help in the development of a system model or may simply be creative in the use of diagrammatic representations.

7. During feasibility analysis, the analyst _____.
   a. considers the educational background and organizational positions of employees
   b. lists file and data base specifications
   c. designs the layout of the screen design for input
   d. prepares the decision logic table

---

a. The analyst asks if the system is practical, cost-effective, feasible, and so on, and in doing so, must review constraints such as this one.

8. The testing and debugging of a system _____.
   a. should take place at all levels of operation
   b. need only be done at the level of the logical modules because they are all independent
   c. is required only if errors appear in reports
   d. is best left to the clerks who will be using the system

a. Programs are tested by dividing them into logical modules. After program testing is complete, system testing checks all application and clerical procedures.

9. Converting only a small portion of the organization to the new system is an example of _____ conversion.

    a. phased   c. pilot

    b. parallel   d. direct

---

c. Pilot conversion minimizes the risk to the organization because unforeseen problems can be identified and corrected before the system is implemented throughout the organization.

10. After a system has been installed, _____.

    a. nothing more needs to be done

    b. it must be maintained continually

    c. the analyst begins the training phase

    d. the analyst prepares the system design report

---

b. System maintenance detects and corrects errors, meets new information needs of management, and responds to changes in the environment.

❏ TRUE/FALSE

1. T F The first step of system design is to formulate a statement of overall business objectives— the goals of the system.

2. T F Only the analyst should be aware that an audit is taking place.

3. T F Questionnaires are an important source of informal data that might not be discovered by other methods of data gathering.

4. T F During data analysis, the analyst may build grid charts or system flowcharts.

5. T F The system analyst proceeds to the detailed system design only if management approves the system design report.

6. T F In the design phase, the analyst concentrates on how a system can be developed to meet information requirements.

7. T F The users of system are not a significant factor in designing the system.

8. T F The decision logic table lists conditions and actions.

9. T F When preparing the design report, the analyst should avoid suggesting any of the alternatives.

10. T F Programmers are usually required to include extensive edit checks on data before storing it in data files.

❏ MATCHING

a. user-friendly	f. direct
b. decision logic table	g. condition
c. menu-driven	h. grid chart
d. system flowchart	i. phased
e. action	j. edit check

1. The diagram used to summarize the relationships among the components of a system is the _____.

2. Emphasis on the flow of data through the entire data-processing system is depicted in a(n) _____.

3. A tabular representation of the actions to be taken under various sets of conditions are displayed on a(n) _____.

4. Implementing a system a portion at a time throughout the entire organization is called _____ conversion.

5. The response to a situation in a decision logic table is depicted by a(n) _____ entry.

6. In a decision logic table, the _____ entry is a situation possibility.

7. A system that fulfills needs through an easy-to-use understandable design is called a(n) _____ system.

8. A system that displays lists of available choices or actions to the user is known as a(n) _____ system.

9. Potential errors in the input data are identified by a(n) _____ processing statement.

10. Implementing a new system all at once is called _____ conversion.

1. What is the first step of system analysis and why is it important?

2. Name some reasons for conducting system analysis.

3. Name four internal sources of data gathering.

4. What are three techniques used to analyze data?

5. What is a system analysis report?

6. How is system design different from system analysis?

7. What are some normal constraints in any organization?

8. Why is it not always necessary for positive economic benefits to exist for an alternative to be feasible?

9. What three classifications of documentation describe a system?

10. What are four approaches to system conversion?

CHAPTER 15

Management Information Systems and Decision Support Systems

❑ KEY TERMS

Centralized design An information structure in which a separate data-processing department is used to provide data-processing facilities for the entire organization.

Decentralized design An information structure in which the authority and responsibility for computer support are placed in relatively autonomous organizational operating units.

Decision support system (DSS) An integrated system that draws on data from a wide variety of sources such as data bases to provide a supportive tool for managerial decision making; generally, accessed by using fourth-generation programming languages.

Distributed design An information structure in which independent operating units have some data-processing facilities, but there is still central control and coordination of computer resources.

Hierarchical design An information structure in which each level within an organization has necessary computer power; responsibility for control and coordination goes to the top level.

Management information system (MIS) A system designed to provide information used to support structured managerial decision making; its goal is to get the correct information to the appropriate manager at the right time.

Model A mathematical representation of an actual system containing independent variables that influence the value of a dependent variable.

Simultaneous decision support system (corporate planning model) A decision support system that attempts to incorporate into one system the decision making of various functional areas of an organization so that management can make consistent, overall decisions.

❑ SUMMARY

Information is data that has been processed and is useful in decision making. Management information systems are information systems that have been designed to provide information to support decision making. In data processing, the emphasis is on short-term or daily operations and on providing detailed information. An MIS, on the other hand, provides summarized information. The goal of MIS is to get the correct information to the manager at the right time in a useful form, and the emphasis is on intermediate and long-range planning.

Most organizations have three levels of management: top-level, middle-level, and lower-level. Each level has different information needs. Top-level managers are concerned with strategic decision making. Activities are future-oriented and involve a great deal of uncertainty. Middle-level managers are concerned with tactical decision making. Activities are required that implement the strategies determined at the top-level. Decision making pertains to control and short-run planning. The lowest-level (first-line supervisors and foreman) makes decisions to ensure that specific jobs are done.

Information must be tailored for each of the three management levels. Lower-level decisions are routine and well-defined and the information can be provided by normal data processing. Middle-level decisions require use of internal information and rapid processing and retrieval of data. Problems lie with meeting needs of top-level management. Top-level problems are nonrepetitive, have a great deal of impact on the organization, and involve uncertainty.

Information for decision making is provided by different types of reports. Scheduled listings are produced at regular intervals and provide routine information to a wide variety of users. Exception reports are generated when there is a deviation from the expected results. Predictive reports are used for planning, and involve "what if" queries. Demand reports, often requested and displayed on a computer terminal, are produced only on request.

An MIS can help management make decisions, but there can be problems. Managers may request too much information, which results in information overload and trouble distinguishing between relevant and irrelevant information. Also, managers often have unrealistic expectations of a system. They may resist computers taking over the decision making.

Structured MIS design methodology attempts to achieve greater productivity by changing the way things are done. Top-down design approaches MIS development by breaking a system down into logical functions, or modules. The main module is the most general level of organization. Each subordinate level becomes increasingly more detailed.

The development of an MIS is an integrated approach to organizing a company's activities. The four basic, but not mutually exclusive, design structures are centralized, hierarchical, distributed, and decentralized. In centralized design, the EDP group controlls computer power. In the hierarchical design, each management level is given the computer power necessary for the tasks. The distributed design breaks the organization into the smallest activity centers requiring computer support. The decentralized design has no central control point.

An MIS supplies managers with information to support structured decision making. It tells a manager what has already happened. A decision support system (DSS) is related to an MIS, but helps with relatively unstructured decisions. A DSS enables a manager to consider more alternatives and can be used to determined what might happen as the result of a certain action. It can aid management in decision making, but cannot make the actual recommendation. A DSS enhances a management information system. Many people believe a DSS is a subsystem of MIS.

A DSS uses models as mathematical representations of the actual system. In the model, independent input variables produce dependent output variables, which helps present the relationships to the manager. Each manager must have a decision model based on his or her perception of the system. DSSs can be purchased from a vendor, or developed from electronic spreadsheet software or expert system shells.

The key factor in the acceptance of a DSS is management attitude. The full potential of a DSS cannot be realized unless obstacles such as management resistance are overcome. To reach this goal, the trend is toward use of simultaneous decision support systems, which combine into one system the functional areas of an organization that affect the performance of other areas.

❑ STRUCTURED LEARNING

1. An MIS is easiest to develop at the lowest level of management because_____.
   a. the organization faces an immediate crisis if the information is faulty at that level
   b. low-level management deals with making tactical decisions
   c. the decisions at this level pertain to control and short-run planning
   d. decisions at this level are generally routine and well defined

d. The information needed at this level is fairly basic and the operations are structured. Lower-level managers are concerned with keeping results in line with plans set by higher levels of management.

2. The emphasis in data processing is on _____.
   a. the short-term operations of a company   c. strategic planning
   b. long-term planning   d. decision making

a. The emphasis is on daily operation of an organization; data processing provides detailed kinds of information.

3. Top-level managers are concerned with _____.
   a. tactical decision making
   b. decisions that ensure that specific jobs are done
   c. strategic decision making
   d. detailed information

c. Activities at the top level of management are future-oriented and involve a great deal of uncertainty. Goals are established at this level and strategies devised for achieving the goals.

4. The organization faces an immediate crisis if information is faulty at the level of _____.
   a. top management
   b. middle management
   c. lower management
   d. clerks

c. Although this level of decision making is fairly basic, it provides the data-processing foundation for the entire organization. False information used for decision making at higher management levels may create a crisis, but the crisis would probably take longer to develop.

5. "What if" kinds of queries are possible with _____.
   a. predictive reports
   b. demand reports
   c. exception reports
   d. scheduled listings

a. Predictive reports are used for planning. The usefulness of these reports depends on how well they can predict future events.

6. Reports that are often requested and displayed on a computer terminal are _____.
   a. predictive reports
   b. demand reports
   c. scheduled listings
   d. exception reports

b. Demand reports are produced only on request. Since they are not required on a continuing basis, they are often requested and displayed on a computer terminal.

7. A problem that arises with an MIS when a manager lacks precise ideas of what information is needed is _____.
   a. improper computer queries
   b. that programs need to be rewritten
   c. communication breakdown
   d. an overload of information

d. Without precise ideas of what is needed, managers often request everything the computer can provide. Then they often cannot distinguish between what is relevant and what is not.

8. The design structure least compatible with the MIS concept is the _____ design.
   - a. hierarchical
   - b. centralized
   - c. distributed
   - d. decentralized

d. Authority and responsibility for computer support are in relatively autonomous organizational operating units and communication among units is limited or nonexistent, thereby ruling out the possibility of common or shared applications.

9. A decision support system helps managers to _____.
   - a. make reports more timely
   - b. determine what might happen
   - c. provide detailed reports
   - d. do their own data retrieval

b. DSS provides managers with information to support relatively unstructured decisions that require a degree of foresight.

10. One of the key factors in the acceptance of decision support systems is _____.
   - a. the eventual lower cost
   - b. the model
   - c. the analyst's attitude
   - d. the attitude of management

d. For the full potential of DSS to be realized, obstacles such as management resistance must be overcome. Managers who fear the erosion of their authority by computers may resist a DSS.

❏ TRUE/FALSE

1. T F   The emphasis in an MIS is on intermediate- and long-range planning.

2. T F   An organization generally has three levels of management.

3. T F   The function of top-level management is keeping the results in line with plans and taking corrective action.

4. T F   As information moves upward in the levels of management, details are weeded out.

5. T F   Reports that ignore normal events are called exception reports.

6. T F   Reports that tend to contain an overabundance of data are demand reports.

7. T F   Top-down design used in designing an MIS involves working on the overview first.

8. T F Standardized classes of hardware, common data bases, and coordinated system development is often seen in the distributed design to MIS.

9. T F A powerful DSS should automate a manager's decision making.

10. T F The use of computers in management can cause problems because promises of what can be accomplished are often unrealistic.

❑ MATCHING

a. top-down	f. lower-level
b. middle-level	g. corporate planning model
c. hierarchical	h. scheduled listings
d. MIS	i. model
e. DSS	j. centralized

1. An information system designed to provide information to support decision making is called a(n) _____.

2. First-line supervisors and foremen are members of _____ management.

3. Managers concerned with tactical decision making are in _____ management.

4. Reports produced at regular intervals that provide routine information to a wide variety of users are called _____.

5. The approach to design that simplifies a system by breaking it into logical modules is _____.

6. A design in which all program development is controlled by the EDP group is _____.

7. The use of varying degrees of responsibility and decision-making authority is typical of a(n) _____ design.

8. Information to support relatively unstructured decisions comes from a(n) _____.

9. A(n) _____ is a mathematical representation of an actual system.

10. The goal of a(n) _____ is to combine into one system the various functional areas of an organization that affect other functional areas.

❏ SHORT ANSWER

1. What is the goal of an MIS?

2. Describe the activities at the top level of management.

3. What is the function of lower-level management?

4. Why is it difficult to design MIS for top-level management?

5. Describe predictive reports. What management level benefits most from their use?

6. Why do some people have unrealistic expectations for an MIS?

7. To what do the four basic design structures (centralized, hierarchical, distributed, and decentralized) apply?

8. What is the main difference between MIS and DSS?

9. What are some obstacles to the realization of the full potential of DSS?

10. Why is the implementation of DSS so difficult?

CHAPTER 16

The Impact of Computers
on People and Organizations

❑ **KEY TERMS**

Audio conferencing A conference call that links three or more people.

Augmented audio conferencing A form of teleconferencing that combines graphics and audio conferencing.

CAD/CAM The combination of computer-aided design and computer-aided manufacturing with which an engineer can analyze not only a product but also the manufacturing process.

Computer anxiety (computerphobia) A fear individuals have of the effects computers have on their lives and society in general.

Computer-aided design (CAD) Process of designing, drafting, and analyzing a prospective product using computer graphics on a video terminal.

Computer-aided manufacturing (CAM) Use of a computer to simulate or monitor the steps of a manufacturing process.

Computer conferencing A form of teleconferencing that uses computer terminals for the transmission of messages; participants need not be using the terminal in order to receive the message_it will be waiting the next time they use the terminal.

Computer-integrated manufacturing (CIM) An arrangement that links various departments within an organization to a central data base for the purpose of improving the efficiency of the manufacturing process.

Electronic mail (e-mail) The transmission of messages at high speeds over telecommunication facilities.

Ergonomics The study of researching and designing computer hardware, software, and work environments to improve employee productivity and comfort.

Facsimile system (FAX system) System that produces a picture of a page by scanning it.

Nondestructive testing (NDT)   Testing done electronically to avoid breaking, cutting, or tearing apart a product to find a problem.

Numerically controlled machinery   Manufacturing machinery that is driven by a magnetic punched tape created by a tape punch that is driven by computer software.

Office automation   Integration of computer and communication technology with traditional office procedures to increase productivity and efficiency.

Robotics   Science that deals with robots and their construction, capabilities, and applications.

Telecomputing   A term referring to the use of online information services that offer access to one or more data bases; for example, CompuServe, The Source, and Dow Jones News/Retrieval.

Teleconferencing   Method of conducting meetings between two or more remote locations via electronic and/or image-producing facilities.

Video seminar   A form of teleconferencing that employs a one way, full-motion video with two-way radio.

Videoconferencing   A technology that employs a two-way, full-motion video plus a two-way audio system for the purpose of conducting conferences between two remote locations through communication facilities.

Voice message system (VMS) or voice mail   System in which the sender activates a message key on the telephone, dials the receiver's number, and records the message. A button lights on the receiver's phone, and when it is convenient, the receiver can activate the phone and listen to the message.

❑ SUMMARY

Computers greatly affect our lives and world with some benefits to our society and some negative effects. People who fear the effects computers have on their lives and society in general are suffering from computer anxiety or computerphobia. Some of these people tend to resist using the machines because they are intimidated by the machines or the jargon, afraid of making mistakes, or afraid of losing their jobs to computerization. The age of the user or the fear of depersonalization contribute to computerphobia. Gender does not seem to be a factor.

While there is no standard definition of computer literacy, most people feel that being comfortable using computers to solve problems is important. Computer literacy courses teach students about the operation of a computer as well as the effects computers have on society.

Automation of manufacturing and other processes leads to lower costs and greater efficiency, but has also eliminated jobs. Generally, new technology creates new employment, which offsets the jobs lost. The extent of displacement depends on several factors including the goals for computer usage, the growth rate of the organization, and the planning that goes into the acquisition and use of the computer.

Computers have caused changes in the workplace, one of which is the issue of health. Ergonomics, a new science concerned with designing hardware, software, and environments that enhance employee comfort and productivity, may help reduce some health concerns.

Office automation refers to procedures that integrate computer and communication technology with the traditional manual processes. It includes word processing, communications, and local area networks. Word processing, the most widely adopted office automation technology, is the manipulation of written text to achieve a desired output. Text can be formatted and revised as needed. Word processors may include such features as spelling checkers, dictionaries, and thesauruses. Communication capabilities made possible through office automation allow the electronic exchange of information between employees through electronic mail, teleconferencing, and telecomputing. Electronic mail is the transmission of messages at high speed over telecommunication facilities. It includes facsimile and voice message systems. Teleconferencing permits two or more locations to communicate via electronic and image-producing facilities. There are several types: audio conferencing, augmented audio conferencing, computer conferencing, video seminars, and videoconferencing. Companies may also subscribe to online information services offering access to one or more data bases. Using these services is called telecomputing.

Computers have greatly affected business and industry by speeding operations, reducing mistakes, and increasing efficiency. Areas where computers are frequently used include accounting and finance, management, and marketing and sales. General accounting software prepares forms and uses spreadsheets. Computers help managers make decisions with a minimum of data. Computers facilitate sales, update inventories, and make projections.

Industry uses computers to design and manufacture products with CAD/CAM, CIM, nondestructive testing, and robotics. Computer-aided design (CAD) enables the engineer to design and analyze a product using computer graphics. CAD is often coupled with computer-aided manufacturing (CAM) to analyze not only the product, but also the manufacturing process. CAM detects major problems as well as controls the machines in manufacturing a product. Manufacturers are combining CAD/CAM with computer-integrated manufacturing (CIM) in an attempt to link various departments of a company into a central data base. The CIM system would control the design and manufacture process from raw materials to finished product.

Nondestructive testing (NDT) combines x-rays, high-frequency sound waves, or laser beams with powerful microcomputers to inspect the interior of a product. This locates possible flaws while leaving the product intact.

Robotics, a term popularized by science fiction writer Isaac Asimov, is the science that deals with robots, their construction, capabilities, and applications. Robots are sometimes called steel-collar workers. The first generation of robots had mechanical dexterity. Second-generation robots also possess some vision and tactile sense.

❏ STRUCTURED LEARNING

1. Computer literacy is a general knowledge about computers that may result in _____.
   a. job displacement
   b. a study of the growth rate of organizations
   c. depersonalization
   d. an understanding about the effects of computer use on society

---

d. It also may include some programming, history of computer development, current uses of computers, practice with software, and projected future trends.

2. After a company installs computer automation, the effect to which job displacement occurs depends on _____.
   a. the fear of unemployment   c. computer anxiety
   b. the growth rate of the organization   d. ergonomics

---

b. If an organization is expanding, it can absorb the displaced workers in other capacities. Other factors are the goals that are sought from the use of computers and the planning that has gone into the acquisition and use of computers.

3. Finding ways of dealing with poor lighting, the noise level of printers, and the layout of keyboards is characteristic of the research in the field of _____.
   a. office automation   c. ergonomics
   b. depersonalization   d. computer literacy

---

c. Ergonomics deals with the development of software, hardware, and environments to increase productivity and comfort among employees.

4. The most widely adopted office automation technology is _____.
   a. electronic conferencing   c. word processing
   b. voice mail   d. electronic spreadsheets

---

c. Word processing, the manipulation of written text to achieve a desired output, bypasses the difficulties and shortcomings of traditional writing and typing. An estimated 75 percent of U.S. companies employ some type of word processing.)

5. A disadvantage of word processing is _____.
    a. the increase of preparation time
    b. the whole document must be retyped for revisions
    c. a modem is required
    d. the increase in the number of times a document is revised

d. It is so easy to change a document, personnel make changes more often than when documents were prepared manually.

6. A possibility in future word processing is _____.
    a. enabling revisions   c. text formatting
    b. thesauruses   d. grammar checkers

d. In the future, grammar checkers may be as common to word processors as spelling checkers are today.

7. The primary purpose of communication capabilities in office automation is _____.
    a. video conferencing
    b. electronic exchange of information between employees
    c. text formatting
    d. to enable two users to manipulate the same screen at once

b. Communication forms are electronic mail, teleconferencing, and telecomputing, and they are an important benefit of office automation.

8. Teleconferencing with two-way, full motion video plus a two-way audio system is called _____.
    a. audio conferencing   c. video seminars
    b. computer conferencing   d. videoconferencing

d. Videoconferencing provides the most effective simulation of face-to-face communication. It is best suited to planning groups, project teams, and other groups that want a full sense of participation.

9. A process that combines X rays, high-frequency sound waves, or laser beams with microcomputers to inspect the interior of a product is called _____.

    a. CAD   c. CIM

    b. CAM   d. NDT

---

d. NDT (nondestructive testing) locates the trouble while leaving the product intact. The process can detect the difference between dangerous flaws and harmless nicks.

10. Computer graphics are helpful to managers because _____.

    a. managers do not like data

    b. graphically displayed data makes decision making much easier

    c. the computer can indicate the solution

    d. graphics are more easily produced than data

---

b. Finding the 20 percent of data necessary for decision making can be difficult for managers if they are presented with pages and pages of data. A graph can be used to summarize large volumes of information.

❏ TRUE/FALSE

1. T F Computers have had only positive effects on our society.

2. T F After a document has been prepared with a word processor, it can be stored on a disk or printed.

3. T F An advantage of word processing–making changes easily–is ironically also a disadvantage of word processing.

4. T F Using online services usually requires a membership fee, a password, and an account number.

5. T F Videoconferencing may be cost effective of a company has major offices throughout the country.

6. T F A problem with nondestructive testing is that it cannot detect the difference between dangerous flaws and minor ones.

7. T F General accounting software was the first business software offered for personal computers.

8. T F The ideal CIM system would control design and manufacture from raw materials to finished product.

9. T F The construction industry is the leading user of robots in the United States.

10. T F NDT could be useful in testing new construction materials.

❏ MATCHING

a. electronic mail
b. telecomputing
c. ergonomics
d. nondestructive testing
e. network

f. augmented audio
g. computer-integrated manufacturing
h. facsimile system
i. robotics
j. office automation

1. The results of radiology and ultrasound tests are processed by computer in a technology known as _____.

2. Researching and designing hardware and software to enhance employees' productivity is known as _____.

3. The process that integrates computer and communication technology with office processes is called _____.

4. The transmission of messages at high speed over telecommunication facilities is _____.

5. A form of electronic mail that transmits across telephone lines using a scanning device is a(n) _____.

6. The form of teleconferencing that combines graphics with audio conferencing is _____.

7. The science that deals with the construction, capabilities, and applications of robots is called _____.

8. The linking of CPUs and terminals by a communication system is called a(n) _____.

9. Subscribing to online information services that offer access to data bases is _____.

10. An attempt to link various departments of a company into a central data base is _____.

1. What are two factors that contribute to computerphobia?

2. What factors determine the extent of job displacement due to technology?

3. How could computer literacy reduce computer anxiety?

4. Name three forms of electronic office communication.

5. Distinguish between computer conferencing and audio conferencing.

6. Why is the study of ergonomics important to people who work with computers?

7. Explain the domino effect in computer business applications.

8. Explain what CAD/CAM does in industry.

9. What is the relationship between NDT and computers?

10. Suggest some factors that would make a computer workstation more ergonomically correct.

CHAPTER 17

Computer Security, Crime, Ethics, and the Law

❑ KEY TERMS

Breach of contract The instance when goods fail to meet the terms of either an express or an implied warranty.

Common law Law that is based on customs and past judicial decisions in similar cases.

Computer crime A criminal act that poses a greater threat to a computer user than to a non-computer user, or a criminal act that is accomplished through the use of a computer.

Computer ethics A term used to refer to the standard of moral conduct in computer use; a way in which the spirit of some laws is applied to computer-related activities.

Computer security The institution of technical and administrative safeguards needed to protect a computer-based system against the hazards to which computer systems are exposed and to control access to information.

Decrypted data Data that is translated back into regular text after being encrypted for security reasons.

Encrypted data A term for data that is translated into a secret code for security reasons.

Express warranty Created when the seller makes any promise or statement of fact concerning the goods being sold, which the purchaser uses as a basis for purchasing the goods.

Hacking A term used to describe the activity of computer enthusiasts who are challenged by the practice of breaking computer security measures designed to prevent unauthorized access to a particular computer system.

Implied warranty A warranty that provides for the automatic inclusion of certain warranties in a contract for the sale of goods.

Implied warranty of fitness A situation in which the purchaser relies on a seller's expertise to recommend a good that will meet the purchaser's needs; if the good later fails to meet the purchaser's needs, the seller has breached the warranty.

Implied warranty of merchantability   Guarantees the purchaser that the good purchased will function properly for a reasonable period of time.

Piracy (software copying)   The unauthorized copying of a copyrighted computer program.

Privacy   An individual's right regarding the collection, processing, storage, dissemination, and use of data about his or her personal attributes and activities.

Public-domain software   Programs unprotected by copyright law; for free, unrestricted public use.

Shareware   Programs that are distributed to the public; the author retains the copyright to the programs with the expectation that users will make donations to the author based upon the value of the program to the users.

Uniform Commercial Code (UCC)   A set of provisions proposed by legal experts to promote consistency among state courts in the legal treatment of commercial transactions between sellers and purchasers.

Virus   A form of sabotage; a computer program that acts as a time bomb that can destroy the contents of a hard or floppy disk.

❑ SUMMARY

Computers are the main means of storing personal information on credit, employment, taxes, etc., making privacy, security, and computer crime growing concerns. The earliest known case of computer crime occurred in 1958. Today, computer crime totals in the billions of dollars. Computer crime consists of two kinds of activities: the use of a computer for acts of theft, deceit, or concealment, and threats to the computer itself such as sabotage or theft of hardware or software. The categories of computer crime are sabotage, theft of services, property crime, and financial crimes.

Sabotage results in destruction or damage to computer hardware, often by former employees or during times of political activism. A virus is a computer program that acts as a time bomb. It can destroy the contents of a hard or floppy disk. Viruses spread through infected disks or through networks. Theft of services means the unauthorized use of computer services, and results from inadequate or nonexistent security. Theft of property occurs when users or employees order merchandise through dummy accounts, copy software, or issue checks paying for nonexistent merchandise. Financial crime involves monetary loss through the issuing of multiple checks for the amount of a single payment, round-off fraud, and data manipulation for clients seeking loads. Government agencies and banks frequently are the victims.

Although computers are often used to commit crime, they can help prevent and detect crime. The Department of Justice keeps files on thousands of persons who could be a threat to government officials.

Extensive data bases can also lead to a suspected person and a solved crime. Some people fear that such files could damage the reputation of an innocent person.

Computer security involves the technical and administrative safeguards to protect a computer-based system. Physical threats to security include fire, natural disasters, environmental problems, and sabotage. Data must also be protected against illegitimate use. Some protection methods include making backup copies, issuing passwords, limiting access to data by users, implementing internal security forces, encrypting data, and using fingerprint or voice detection.

Sometimes companies are unwilling to report problems with security, fearing bad publicity. Thus, users need to be trained to respect their roles in security. A company should have a well-trained security force to scrutinize the system and the data for problems. New employees should be screened, and unethical employees discharged.

Users should maintain the standard of moral conduct called computer ethics in questionable situations. For example, hacking is often considered harmless, but can be a serious crime. Employees owe a measure of loyalty to their employers regarding confidential information. The unauthorized copying of a copyrighted program is a crime, even on a small scale.

The electronic invasion of individual privacy is a major concern. Personal information is easy to obtain and there is less control over data in computer files. Incorrect information can be hard to change. There must be a balance between how much information an organization needs about an individual and the person's right to privacy. Numerous laws have been passed since the early 1970s to stop computer information abuse and protect rights to privacy. The Privacy Act of 1974 is one of the most important. It states that people may know what is recorded about them, that inaccurate data must be correctable, that data can only be used for one purpose, and that stored information must be reliable. Other laws have passed further defining these rights. State laws are patterned after federal law and tend to be similar.

There are legal issues involved with owning a computer system, too. The Uniform Commercial Code (UCC) and common law govern warranty cases. Express warranties are created when the seller makes any promise or statement of fact concerning goods sold. A breach of contract of the expressed warranty can result in a reduction in the price or replacement of the product. Implied warranties are automatic warranties that exist by law. Two major types are implied warranty of merchantability and implied warranty of fitness.

Copyrights protect the writer of programs from actions by the buyers. Current law protects against unauthorized copying of software. It protects the computer program, but not the ideas and methods for creating the program. Site licenses are available to users who want to use a program on multiple systems.

Public-domain software is not copyright protected. Such software is obtainable from online services. Shareware is copyrighted software that the author allows the public to copy. The source code is not distributed and users donate a sum to the author based on the value of the program to the users.

❏ STRUCTURED LEARNING

1. Computer sabotage _____.
   a. requires sophisticated knowledge of the computer
   b. has not been a serious problem
   c. often resembles traditional sabotage
   d. cannot be detected until files are opened

c. Sabotage results in destruction or damage of computer hardware. No special expertise is needed unless computer-assisted security must be thwarted.

2. "Round-off fraud" is a type of _____.
   a. financial crime
   b. property theft
   c. sabotage
   d. erasing of data using magnets

a. It involves collecting the fractions of cents in customers' accounts that are created when the applicable interest rates are figured.

3. The FBI has been criticized for its crime predictor files because _____.
   a. it doesn't help detect criminals
   b. the FBI will not let anyone see them
   c. prisons have access to the files
   d. the data could harm an innocent person

d. Some fear the Justice Department may use the system to monitor people who are considered a threat to officials, but who have never been convicted of a crime, thereby abusing the purpose of the system.

4. The best way to extinguish a fire in the computer room is with _____.
   a. water
   b. halon, a nonpoisonous chemical gas
   c. a carbon dioxide fire extinguisher
   d. foam

b. Halon extinguishers are expensive, but water can damage magnetic storage media and carbon dioxide can endanger employees.

5. Internal sabotage, fraud, and embezzlement are often not reported because the company that falls victim to these crimes _____.
    a. fears bad publicity
    b. normally fires the employee
    c. solves the crime without police help
    d. feels it is not worth the effort to report the crime

---

a. Banks and insurance companies are especially susceptible to crime by employees. Such crimes are also difficult to solve and tend to undermine the confidence of the public.

6. The term used to describe the activity of computer enthusiasts who are challenged by the practice of breaking computer security measures is _____.
    a. encryption   c. hacking
    b. decryption   '   d. piracy

---

c. Hacking is considered a criminal act. Gaining unauthorized access to someone's computer can be as serious as breaking into someone's home.

7. Authors of shareware retain _____ to their work.
    a. the expressed warranty   c. price controls
    b. the copyright   d. the implied warranty

---

b. Authors of shareware make their programs available to the public with the idea that the user will make donations to the author. The source code is generally not distributed with the program and the author retains copyright to the program.

8. Much of the federal government's information for its data bases comes from _____.
    a. census returns and income tax returns   c. libraries and online services
    b. government employee surveys   d. schools and private business

---

a. Other information sources include the Department of Transportation, Veterans' Administration, social security, and welfare recipients.

9. Taking someone to court for invasion of privacy is a problem because _____.
   a. courts generally won't define "invasion of privacy"
   b. each state has its own laws regarding invasion of privacy
   c. lawyers cannot get the proof because to do so would be an invasion of privacy
   d. more private aspects could be exposed in court than the original intrusion

---

d.   A problem of privacy violation is that data is used without the subjects knowing that it was used so the victim may not realize a privacy violation has occurred.

10. In order to make a software package on a network accessible to more than one user at a time, a company may need to acquire a(n) _____.
   a. copyright   c. electronic bulletin board
   b. express warranty   d. site license

---

d.   A site license permits multiple users of the single copy of a program installed on a network.

❑ TRUE/FALSE

1. T F Wiretapping onto a user's line is often used to gain access to a time-sharing system.

2. T F Criminals can conceal their identities and the existence of the crime in computer financial crimes.

3. T F Water and steam pipes, magnetic fields, and power failures are some environmental threats to computers.

4. T F There are no laws against the unethical activities of hackers.

5. T F Companies have found that employees who commit fraud should be retained to help tighten security.

6. T F Courts have held that employee loyalty has no place in the computer field because there is too much job changing.

7. T F The solution to the privacy issue must be a balance between the needs of the organization and the rights of individuals.

8. T F Most laws protecting privacy are to prevent abuse by the federal government's record-keeping agencies.

9. T F Federal laws against computer crime were enacted because state laws were too vague and dissimilar.

10. T F Current copyright law does not protect against unauthorized use, only unauthorized copying.

❏ MATCHING

a. implied warranties
b. encrypted
c. breach of contract
d. shareware
e. piracy

f. computer security
g. public-domain
h. privacy
i. computer ethics
j. hacking

1. The technical and administrative safeguards required to protect a computer-based system are known as _____.

2. Data translated into a secret code is _____.

3. The standard of moral conduct in computer use is called _____.

4. The activity of computer enthusiasts who break computer security measures is called _____.

5. The unauthorized copying of a computer program that has been written by someone else is known as _____.

6. An individual's ability to determine what, how, and when personal information is given to others is called _____.

7. If goods sold fail to conform to the express warranty, a(n) _____ occurs.

8. When a contract for the sale of goods automatically contains certain warranties that exist by law it is called a(n) _____.

9. The software that is unprotected by copyright law is called _____ software.

10. The user normally gives a donation to the author of _____.

1. Define computer crime.

2. What are the categories of computer crime?

3. What are some hazards to computer systems?

4. What is decryption?

5. What protection does the Privacy Act of 1974 offer?

6. What is the difference between the UCC and common law?

7. When does the UCC apply to computer transactions?

8. What are express warranties?

9. What is an implied warranty of merchantability?

10. What is an implied warranty of fitness?

CHAPTER 18

Computers in Our Lives: Today and Tomorrow

❏ KEY TERMS

Artificial intelligence Field of research currently developing techniques whereby computers can be used to solve problems that appear to require imagination, intuition, or intelligence.

Computer-assisted instruction (CAI) Use of a computer to instruct or drill a student on an individual or small-group basis.

Computerized axial tomography (CT or CAT) scanning Form of noninvasive physical testing that combines X-ray techniques and computers to aid diagnosis.

Dynamic random-access memory (DRAM) chip The type of memory chip used in most personal computers; it must constantly be refreshed; pronounced dee-ram.

Expert system Form of artificial intelligence software designed to imitate the same decision-making and evaluation processes of experts on a specific field.

Fiber optics A data transmission concept using laser pulses and cables made of tiny threads of glass than can transmit huge amounts of data accurately and at the speed of light.

Fuzzy logic Logic that allows for imprecision based on rules that set ranges for characteristics.

Interactive video A multimedia learning concept that merges computer text, sound, and graphics by using a videodisk, videodisk player, microcomputer with monitor and disk drive, and computer software.

Multimedia Computer applications that combine audio and video components with interactive applications.

Multiphasic health testing (MPHT) Computer-assisted testing plan that compiles data on patients and their test results, which are compared with norms or means to aid the physician in making a diagnosis.

Neural network A type of software or hardware that attempts to imitate the way the brain works by creating connections for nodes and units in the system.

Nonmonotonic logic   A type of logic that adapts to exceptions to ordinary monotonic logical statements and allows conclusions to be drawn from assumptions.

Nuclear magnetic resonance (NMR)   A computerized, noninvasive diagnostic tool that involves sending magnetic pulses through the body to identify medical problems.

Parallel processing   A type of processing in which instructions and data are handled simultaneously.

Script theory   A theory used in the research of artificial intelligence (AI) that is based on the concept that any circumstance can be described by a script. For example, each person may have a dentist office script, a classroom script, and a restaurant script. These scripts shape a person's behavior and influence how he or she may react in similar situations. Script theory attempts to apply this logic to computers so that they may "think" like humans.

Virtual reality   A computer system including hardware and software that enables a person to experience and manipulate a three-dimensional world that exists only in projected images.

❏ SUMMARY

In forty-five years the computer industry has moved from vacuum tubes to research in molecular electronics and optical computers. The first integrated circuit was produced by Jack Kilby in 1958. Today millions of circuits are crowded on silicon chips. This results in problems of heat and cross talk. Gallium arsenide and multichip modules overcome some of the problems inherent in silicon chips. Some scientists believe they can grow chips from organic matter, too.

Fiber optics and laser technology aid computer technology in an important way. The tiny glass fibers carry digital signals at very fast rates. Lasers are also used in chip production and may be part of an actual computer in the future.

Parallel processing, rather than the current serial processing, will further increase the speed of computers without miniaturization. It imitates the brain by dividing a problem into several portions and processing the portions simultaneously using two or more microprocessors.

Computers are best at handling huge amounts of numerical data, often called number crunching, but many scientists are working on other applications that require artificial intelligence. AI applies humanlike thinking, common sense, self-teaching, and decision-making skills to machines. Current AI applies only a few aspects of human intelligence in what are known as expert systems. These systems, which are not true AI, imitate an expert in the field, drawing conclusions and making recommendations to reduce options and uncertainty. Other approaches to AI are nonmonotonic logic, which allows conclusion to be drawn from assumptions, and script theory, which uses common sense to make inferences about a situation.

Advanced AI could be applied to voice recognition and robotics. Current voice-recognition systems are limited and expensive. Robots are limited in vision, touch, mobility, and methods of instruction. For robots to do more human jobs, they need sophisticated sensors for touch, depth vision, sensors to maintain balance while walking, and an adequate way to receive instructions, learn new tasks, and make simple decisions.

Computers, combined with testing equipment, provide tools for medicine. Multiphasic health testing aids in testing, stores the results, and reports the results to doctors. Computerized axial tomography (CAT scanning) uses X rays to produce three-dimensional pictures of organs or bones. Nuclear magnetic resonance (NMR) may replace CAT because it uses magnetic pulses instead of radiation. These diagnostic techniques avoid the risks involved in exploratory surgery. Computers can also aid in treatment. Microprocessors are applied to heart pacemakers and artificial limbs, and they are used to control the release of medication. Computers control lasers in surgery on tumors or kidney stones.

In other areas of science, computers help scientists do calculations, simulations, and observations. They monitor the environment, chemical industries, nuclear power plants, and weather. The National Weather Service is upgrading its equipment so that it can more adequately predict severe weather such as tornadoes. It is using computers for analyzing the data and creating numerical models that condense data into graphic form. Computers also keep watch on volcanoes, measuring crater floor tilt, and tremors. They can predict eruptions within 30 minutes. Earthquakes are, as yet, not so easy to predict, but computer technology is helping scientists develop sophisticated models for this use.

In the near future, computers will allow new technologies in the home. Future homes will be labor and energy savers and help handicapped people. The computers will be powerful, use little energy, do banking transactions, offer college courses, and accept commands in English. Even the appliances will be run by microprocessors that use fuzzy logic, which quantifies concepts such as pretty hot, somewhat heavy, and so on.

Interactive video will be used in homes, schools, and training. It merges graphics and sound with computer-generated text by linking an optical disk, a videodisk player, a microcomputer, and software. The interactive video generates questions and the user can form inquiries about news footage, historical events, and science. The current term for the multitude of sensory, interactive experiences is multimedia. A multimedia application can be written using an authoring language. Users employ a special type of data base system, called hypertext, to see all the objects related to a particular subject. The ultimate in multimedia is virtual reality, which enables users to work or play in a three-dimensional, realistic world of images.

Some experts believe that every future job will depend on a person's computer knowledge. Others believe computer knowledge for jobs is a myth and that students need reading and thinking skills. Software packages categorized as computer-assisted instruction (CAI) can help students learn skills in a variety of ways. They include drills, tutorials, simulations, games, problem solving software, and multimedia experiences.

❏ STRUCTURED LEARNING

1. Cross talk may result when _____.
   a. the chip overheats
   b. the chip is made of gallium arsenide
   c. circuits are crowded together
   d. multichip modules are used

---

c. Two problems arise when electronic components are crowded together. One is cross talk and the other is heat. Cross talk resembles the problem you may experience when you make a long-distance telephone call and hear another conversation in the background.

2. A technology that may soon carry high-definition television, dial-up encyclopedias, interactive education, and other information services into the home is _____.
   a. parallel processing
   b. multichip modules
   c. DRAMs
   d. fiber optics

---

d. Fiber optic cables carry digital signals and offer very high-speed, accurate transmission.

3. Parallel processing enables _____ to occur.
   a. multiprogramming
   b. multiprocessing
   c. virtual memory
   d. multitasking

---

b. Multiprocessing is the running of more than one instruction simultaneously.

4. A neural network _____.
   a. has no explicit set of rules but makes up its own rules that match the data as it comes in
   b. uses the concepts of script theory
   c. applies the only true form of artificial intelligence
   d. is a refined method of number crunching

---

a. Neural networks can be trained to do a job by being exposed to thousands of samples that demonstrate a range of correct responses to a problem.

5. Perhaps the most crucial problem to overcome in robots is _____.
   a. vision
   b. touch
   c. balance
   d. hearing

a. Robots see in only two dimensions–length and width. Unlike humans, they do not judge depth. Some scientists are designing robots that use fiber optic "eyes" as tiny cameras.

6. A drawback of NMR is _____.
    a. it cannot produce clear images of bones
    b. it uses high levels of radiation
    c. it is too complex for a hospital technician
    d. it involves surgery

a. Nuclear magnetic resonance works without radiation and may soon replace CAT scans. NMR can "see" through thick bones, but cannot spot breast cancer.

7. In order to understand the development of severe weather, scientists are using _____.
    a. seismometers
    b. numerical models
    c. strain meters
    d. fiber optics

b. Scientists are using a new algorithm for condensing data about thunder clouds into graphic forms. These numerical models of thunderstorms can help the scientists understand how thunder clouds spawn tornadoes.

8. A concept that could "tell" a camcorder to adjust the picture when the photographer accidentally jiggles the camera is _____.
    a. interactive video
    b. nonmonotonic logic
    c. virtual reality
    d. fuzzy logic

d. Fuzzy logic quantifies imprecise concepts according to rules that set ranges for characteristics.

9. Authoring tools enable users to write _____.
    a. fuzzy logic applications
    b. robotic programs
    c. multimedia applications
    d. expert systems

c. Authoring tools enable users to create a final application by linking together objects, such as written text, a graph, a drawing, and music or sound effects.

10. A concept that has a great deal of potential for training applications is _____.
   a. fuzzy logic
   c. script theory
   b. virtual reality
   d. NMR

---

b.   Virtual reality allows users to work through procedures in a three-dimensional, realistic way without endangering anyone.

❏ TRUE/FALSE

1. T   F   The use of gallium arsenide as a chip material has fallen out of favor because of its expense.

2. T   F   Parallel processing increases computer speed without further miniaturizing the circuitry.

3. T   F   An expert system is the first true artificial intelligence.

4. T   F   Some robots are built to act according to each new situation encountered.

5. T   F   A CAT scan creates a three-dimensional composite of an organ or bone.

6. T   F   With today's models, scientists are able to predict the time and place of earthquakes accurately.

7. T   F   A computer can generate pictures that show how a person will look after reconstructive surgery.

8. T   F   Experts predict that home use of computers will decline in the future.

9. T   F   CAI includes drills and tutorials.

10. T   F   Some researchers believe that computer education will not be a prerequisite for jobs in the future.

❏ MATCHING

a. script theory
b. multichip modules
c. computer-assisted instruction
d. artificial intelligence
e. computerized axial tomography

f. parallel processing
g. nuclear magnetic resonance
h. expert
i. nonmonotonic logic
j. multiphasic health testing

1. Cross talk can be reduced with the use of _____.

2. Using two or more CPUs to process different portions of a problem simultaneously is known as _____.

3. Humanlike thinking by machines is called _____.

4. Systems that draw conclusions and make recommendations based on heuristics are called _____ systems.

5. Drawing conclusions from assumptions that are not wrong if new assumptions are added is an example of _____.

6. _____ says that in a particular situation, humans have an idea of how the dialogue will go.

7. Using computers to perform medical testing is called _____.

8. X-rays and computerized evaluation of X-ray pictures is known as _____.

9. A scanning device that does not use radiation is _____.

10. Software for teaching is called _____.

❏ SHORT ANSWER

1. What are the two problems of placing electronic components close together?

2. Of what advantage is gallium arsenide in chips used for missile guidance?

3. What are some advantages of data transmission using fiber optics?

4. Why is artificial intelligence so difficult to perfect?

5. What are some of the procedures included in multiphasic health testing?

6. How are CAT scans and NMR better than surgery?

7. What is the current status of voice recognition technology?

8. Name two uses of microprocessors in helping patients with disabilities.

9. Name some types of CAI software.

10. How many years ago was the first integrated circuit introduced?

Word Processors

❏ KEY TERMS

Automatic page numbering A feature that enables a word processor to automatically number the pages of the printed copy.

Block-copy A feature that marks a block of text and duplicates it at a new location.

Block-delete A feature that marks a block of text and then issues a single command to delete the entire block of text.

Block-merge A feature that reads a file from disk and merges it with the document currently in memory.

Block-move A feature that marks a block of text and then moves it from one location to another.

Block-operations A feature that allows the user to define a block of text and then perform a specific operation on the entire block. Common block operations include block move, block copy, block save, and block delete.

Block-save A feature that marks a block of text and saves it as a new file on disk.

Buffer A separate area of memory in which characters can be stored an retrieved; used when transmitting data from one device to another.

Centered text A feature of most word-processing programs that allows you to center a word or line by simply pressing one or two keys.

Cursor The marker on the display screen indicating where the next character can be displayed.

Default setting A value used by the word processor when not instructed to use any other.

Deletion A feature in which a character, word, sentence, or larger block of text may be removed from the existing text.

Disk-based word processor A word processor that loads into memory only the part of the document that is being edited, storing the remainder in temporary disk files.

Document-oriented word processor A word processor that treats a document as a single continuous file.

Editing window The text area of the screen which contains the words as they are typed.

Footer A piece of text that is printed at the bottom of each page, such as a page number.

Global search and replace A feature that finds all occurrences of a word or words and automatically replaces the word with another word or words.

Header A piece of text that is stored separately from the text and printed at the top of each page.

Indent A feature used to indent all lines of a paragraph the same number of spaces from the left margin. This feature is often used for long quotations.

Insert and replace A feature that allows new characters to be entered into a document, replacing old characters.

Line-spacing A feature that lets the user choose the amount of space between lines.

Memory-based word processor A word processor that can only accommodate documents that fit into available memory; longer documents must be placed in two or more separate files.

Page-oriented word processor A word processor that treats a document as a series of pages.

Print-formatting The function of a word processor that communicates with the printer to tell it how to print the text on paper.

Screen-formatting A function of a word processor that controls how the text will appear on the screen.

Screen-oriented word processing A word processor that ideally matches what is seen on the screen with what is printed on paper. See also WYSIWYG.

Scrolling Moving a line of text onto or off the screen.

Search A feature that lets you look for a word or phrase in a document.

Search and replace A feature that finds a certain word or phrase but also lets you replace it with another word or phrase.

Status line A message above or below the text area on a display screen that gives format and system information.

Tab A feature that works the same as the tab key on a typewriter. Options include tabs that place columns of words and numbers to the left, center, or right of the tab setting.

Undo A feature that cancels a command, allowing you to undo what you have done.

Word wrap The feature by which a word is automatically moved to the beginning of the next line if it goes past the right margin.

WYSIWYG A common terms that is used when discussing word processors, pronounced *wizzeewig*. The letters stand for "what you see is what you get." This means that what you see on the screen matches as closely as possible what actually appears when the document is printed.

❏ SUMMARY

Word processors are extremely popular because they are a useful tool for more users than any other application software program and because learning how to use them is easy. The purpose a word processor is to help the user create a good-looking and well-written document.

When using a word processor, the computer screen is usually divided into two areas. The part of the screen that gives information about the status of the program and the format of the document often contains a menu, and a status line. The remainder of the screen, called the editing window, contains words as they are typed.

In a memory-based word processor the entire document must fit into memory. Documents larger than available memory are divided into two or more files. A disk-based word processor loads into memory only the part of the document being edited, storing the remainder in temporary disk files. A page-oriented word processor treats a text files as a series of pages, much like a typewriter. A document-oriented word processors treats a document as a single continuous file.

When considering their uses, there are generally five categories of word processors: personal, professional, corporate, legal, and desktop publishing.

All word processors perform the same basic tasks such as entering, editing, and formatting text, moving blocks of text, searching for and replacing strings of text. Writing and editing features of many word processors include cursor movement, scrolling, insert and replace, word wrap, delete, block operations, undo and search. Screen-formatting features include tabs, indents and page breaks. Print-formatting features include margin settings, headers and footers, page length, automatic page numbering, paragraph layout, paragraph margins, justifying text, line spacing, and character attributes. Other features included in many word processors are help facilities, windows, dictionaries and thesauruses, print merge, hyphenation, sorting, math, drawing, columns, indexing, table of contents and macros.

The basic hardware needed to run a word processor includes the computer, disk drive, monitor, printer, and printer interface card. Current trends in word-processing software include greater specialization, increasing connectivity with other programs such as spreadsheet programs and data managers, and a move toward document processing or the combination of word processing and desktop publishing.

❏ STRUCTURED LEARNING

1. _____ allow manipulation of large numbers of characters at the same time.
   a. word wrap
   b. global search and replace
   c. block operations
   d. character attributes

___

c. block operations such as block-delete, block-move, block copy, block-save and block-merge allow the manipulation of large numbers of characters at the same time.

2. The print merge function typically consists of _____ documents.
   a. one
   b. two
   c. three
   d. four

___

b. Two. The main document contains standard text that remains constant and the merge document contains the text that varies from letter to letter.

3. Document processing is combining word processing with _____.
   a. desktop publishing
   b. spreadsheets
   c. data managers
   d. documents used by lawyers

___

a. Combining word processing with desktop publishing is a popular current trend with the newer word processors.

4. The _____ feature places all lines of a paragraph the same number of spaces in from the left margin.
   a. tab
   b. paragraph layout
   c. line spacing
   d. indent

___

d. The indent feature is often used for lists and long quotations.

5. A _____ allows the user to request the synonyms of any word on the screen.
   a. dictionary
   c. speller
   b. thesaurus
   d. lexicon

---

b. An electronic thesaurus displays synonyms and in some cases antonyms for specific words.

❏ TRUE/FALSE

T F 1. When using a word processor, the return key has to be pressed at the end of every line, just like a typewriter.

T F 2. Word processors today all have only one window.

T F 3. The increased sophistication of word processors has caused the RAM requirements to run them to increase.

T F 4. The indexing feature on some word processors automatically generate an alphabetized index of key words or phrased with their corresponding page numbers.

T F 5. When a word processor is in the typeover mode, new characters are added to the existing text without deleting anything.

❏ MATCHING

a. buffer
b. character attributes
c. macro
d. scrolling
e. justifying

1. _____ include boldface, underline, italics, subscript, and superscript.

2. A _____ is a string of text that has been created and saved in a special file and can be retrieved by pressing a key or a certain key combination.

3. Moving lines of text on and off the screen is called _____.

4. _____ text refers to where text is placed on a line in relationship to the left and right margins.

5. A _____ is a separate area of memory in which characters can be stored and from which they can be retrieved.

1. What is the difference between a page-oriented word processor and a document-oriented word processor?

2. What information is provided in a status line?

3. What are the three processes involved in print-formatting?

4. List the typical block operations.

5. What are the five categories of word processors?

Spreadsheets

❑ KEY TERMS

Cell The unique location in an electronic spreadsheet where a row and a column intersect.

Command area The part of the screen tat shows a menu of the available commands.

Coordinate The location of a cell within a spreadsheet; a combination of the column letter and row number that intersect at a specific cell.

Copy A function that allows the user to copy a cell or group of cells to another part of the spreadsheet.

Electronic spreadsheet An electronic ledger sheet used to store and manipulate any type of numeric data.

Formula A mathematical equation used in a spreadsheet.

Hidden cells A feature that allows the user to hide data in a cell so that the contents are not displayed on the screen.

Labels Information used for describing some aspect of a spreadsheet.

Locked cells A feature that prevents a user from altering or destroying a template by locking the cell with a special command.

Macro A sequence of keystrokes entered into one or more cells that can be activated with a single command that often involves only two keystrokes.

Recalculation A feature that automatically adjusts the result of a formula when a cell used in the formula changes.

Sort A feature used to arrange the records in a file.

Spreadsheet A spreadsheet is a grid of columns and rows used to store and manipulate numeric information. The electronic spreadsheet takes the place of ledger sheets used by accountants.

Status area Lines at either the top or the bottom of the screen make up the status area and provide information about the cell at the cursor's position.

Template In a spreadsheet program, a template is a set of predefined formulas already entered into the spreadsheet so that new figures can be entered without having to reenter the formulas.

Value A single piece of numeric information used in the calculations of a spreadsheet.

Variable column width A software feature that allows the user to set the width of columns.

Window The portion of a worksheet that can be seen on the computer display screen.

❑ SUMMARY

A spreadsheet program is basically a calculator that uses a computer's memory capability to solve mathematically oriented problems. An electronic spreadsheet is a grid of columns and rows used to store and manipulate numeric information. Spreadsheets store not only numbers but also formulas for calculating numbers.

A spreadsheet program can perform complex mathematical calculations. Numbers or values are entered into the cells formed by the columns and rows. Label are used to identify what the numbers mean.

Formulas can also be entered into cells. A formula is a mathematical expression that can contain numbers from other cells. Because of the spreadsheets ability to instantly recalculate a formula if a value in the formula changes they are used to answer "what if" questions, or question that seek to find out what will happen to certain numbers in a spreadsheet if other numbers change.

Each cell in a spreadsheet has a coordinate which consists of a letter for its column and a number for its row.

Businesses often use spreadsheets to keep track of such things as sales figures, expenses, payroll amounts, and prices. Features of spreadsheets include variable column width, automatic spillover, titles, windows, inserting and deleting rows and columns graphics, predefined formulas, locking cells, hiding cells, formatting cells, ranges, copy, recalculation, sorting, functions, macros, file linking and multiple pages.

A current trend in spreadsheet programs is the development of add-in products that are used in conjunction with a spreadsheet program to enhance it.

1. Which one of the following is a coordinate in a spreadsheet?
   a. 6B   c. 870Z
   d. M33   d. M3B

---

d. A coordinate is made up of the column letter and row number that intersect at a specific cell.

2. When a spreadsheet is in the _____ mode, the cursor can be moved around the worksheet.
   a. ready   c. entry
   d. command   d. cursor

---

a. When the spreadsheet is in the entry mode, data is being entered into a cell. Menus listing the available commands are active in the command mode. There is no cursor mode.

3. The _____ feature allows labels that are too long for one cell to go over into the next cell.
   a. titles   c. variable column width
   b. window   d. automatic spillover

---

d. The variable column width feature allows the user to set the width of columns. The title feature shows the labels in a spreadsheet on the screen at all times. The windows feature lets the user divide the screen into miniscreens.

4. A _____ is a set of predefined formulas already entered into a spreadsheet.
   a. template   c. macro
   b. coordinate   d. value

---

a. A coordinate is the location of a cell within a spreadsheet. A value is a single piece of numeric information and a macro is a series of keystrokes that can be activated with a single command.

5. In spreadsheets, the multiple page feature is sometimes referred to as _____.
   a. recalculating pages   c. "3-D" spreadsheets
   b. file linking   d. add-in products

---

c. Multiple pages give a spreadsheet the third dimension of "depth," that is, spreadsheet files can be stacked on top of one another like pages.

❏ TRUE/FALSE

T F 1. Formulas can contain numbers from other cells in the spreadsheet.

T F 2. If a value containing 12 characters is entered into a column with a width of 10 charac-
       ters, the last 2 characters will spill over into the next cell.

T F 3. A range of cells is a rectangular group of calls that is treated as a unit for some operation.

T F 4. The contents of locked cells are not displayed on the screen.

T F 5. Macros can be used to automate most spreadsheet tasks.

❏ MATCHING

    a. functions
    b. file linking
    c. formatting
    d. recalculation
    e. dynamic linking

1. Linking an area in the spreadsheet with an area in a word-processing document is called _____.

2. Linking a cell from one worksheet with a cell from another worksheet is called _____.

3. _____ controls how the contents of a cell are displayed.

4. _____ such as mathematical, statistical, and financial, provide a shortcut to accomplish certain tasks.

5. The _____ feature automatically adjusts the result of a formula when a cell used in the formula
   changes.

❏ SHORT ANSWER

1. What does the term "what if" question mean?

2. List the operations that can be performed on a range of cells.

3. What are the common categories of functions?

4. List the ways macros can be used to automate spreadsheet tasks.

5. Explain what an "add-in" product is.

Data Managers

❏ KEY TERMS

Add A feature that allows you to add another record to an existing file.

Data manager A software package used to organize files that lets you store and access data with your computer.

Data redundancy The repeating of data in different files so that if data changes, it must be updated in all the files in which it occurs.

Delete A feature that allows you to remove or erase a record you no longer want.

Field A meaningful collection of characters, such as a social security number or a person's name.

File A grouping of related records, such as student records; sometimes referred to as a data set.

File manager An application package designed to duplicate the traditional manual methods of filing records.

Index A feature used to maintain ascending or descending order among a list of entries.

Key The unique identifier or field of a record; used to sort records for processing or to locate specific records within a file.

Record A collection of data items, or fields, that relates to a single unit, such as a student.

Relational data base A data base that allows the user to open and use data from several files at one time.

Search A feature that lets you look for a word or phrase in a document.

Sort A feature used to arrange the records in a file.

Update A feature that allows you to change data contained in a record.

❏ Summary

Data managers have more strategic importance to a company than any other business application. Data managers are software packages that computerize record-keeping tasks. A data-manager software package is used to organize files. Each data item is called a field. A group of related fields form a record. A file is a group of related records. Most data managers can add or delete data within a file, search a file for certain data, update or change data in a file, sort data into some order, and print all or part of the data in a file.

File managers were originally developed to replace traditional filing systems. File managers store data in a two dimensional table similar to a spreadsheet. Flat-file data bases can access only one file at a time. Data cannot be pulled from two files into one report. Flat files sometimes have a problem with data redundancy or the repeating of the same data in different files.

The main difference between file managers and relational data bases is that a relational data base can draw from more than one file at a time. Files can be linked through one or more shared relations. A shared relation would be data that is common to all the files such as a common field or fields. Relational data bases reduce data redundancy and make updating a file easier.

Features of data managers include add and delete, search and update, data verification, sort, indexing, print, report generator, query facilities, and the inclusion of programming languages.

Two current trends in data-management software are the increased features and power found in the programs and the move towards using data managers in a distributed processing environment.

❏ Structured Learning

1. A group of related fields form a(n) _____.
   - a. file
   - b. data base
   - c. record
   - d. index

c. A group of related fields form a record. A school may keep a record about each student. Such a record might contain fields such as the student name, home address, grade-point average and so on.

2. Flat files have a tendency to have problems with _____.
   - a. indexing
   - b. data redundancy
   - c. using a lot of the computer's memory
   - d. data verification

b. Data redundancy, the repeating of data in different files, can be a problem with flat files. Since only one file can be open at a time, different files usually have to contain the same information.

3. A(n) _____ is a unique identifier or field of a record which is used to sort records for processing or to locate specific records within a file.
   a. key
   b. index
   c. record manager
   d. report generator

_____

a. An index consists of a list of keys in the desired order and a pointer to the master list.

4. If you wanted to change data contained in a record, you would use the _____ feature.
   a. add
   c. search
   b. delete
   d. update

_____

d. The update feature allows you to change data contained in a record.

5. The _____ feature helps to ensure that the correct data is entered into each field.
   a. search
   c. update
   b. data verification
   d. index

_____

b. There are two methods of data verification that help to ensure the correct data is entered, required fields and defining a field as numeric or character.

❑ TRUE/FALSE

T F   1. Each data item such as a name or the amount of a bill is a file.
T T   2. A flat file data base can only access one file at a time.
T F   3. Relational data bases have problems with data redundancy.
T F   4. Data managers can be used with word processors to produce form letters.
T F   5. Band-oriented report writers are very difficult to use.

❏ MATCHING

    a. distributed processing
    b. QBE
    c. record
    d. report
    e. required

1. A group of related fields in a data base form a _____.

2. The purpose of the _____ generator is to get answers out of the data base.

3. The _____ facility allows the user to ask questions by filling out a table.

4. A _____ field is a method of data verification.

5. The high-level sharing of data and processing power on a network of microcomputers, minicomputers, and mainfraimes, is called _____.

❏ SHORT ANSWER

1. List the tasks most data managers can perform.

2. What is the difference between a file manager and a relational data base?

3. List some of the specialized uses of data managers.

4. What is the difference between indexing and sorting?

5. What are the two classifications of programming languages included with relational data bases and what is the difference between them?

Integrated Software

❑ KEY TERMS

Integrated software Two or more application programs that work together, allowing easy movement of data between the applications; the applications also use a common group of commands.

Stand-alone program A single, self-contained application program that serves one purpose.

Systems integrator An operating environment that makes it possible to move data from one stand-alone program to another. a Systems integrator uses windows to allow the simultaneous operation of stand-alone programs.

Utility program A program within an operating system that performs a specialized function.

❑ SUMMARY

Integrated software is two or more application programs that work together allowing easy movement of data between the applications. Integrated software uses a common group of commands among all the applications.

Integrated software conforms to the following three standards:
1. The software consists of application programs that are usually separate.
2. The software provides easy movement of data among the separate applications.
3. A common group of commands is used for all the applications in the software package.

Applications frequently included in an integrated software package are data managers, spreadsheet analysis, word processing, and graphics. Many integrated software packages also include communications.

There are four types of integrated software. They are:
1. The all-in-one package.
2. The integrated series.
3. The systems integrator.
4. The background utility approach.

Features of integrated software include a help option, windows, and zoom. The popularity of integrated packages has been affected by the availability of add-in products and the move towards software compatibility.

❏ Structured Learning

1. Integrated software attempts to maximize both _____ and _____ compatibility.
   - a. command; data
   - b. software; printer
   - c. hardware; software
   - d. home use; business use

---

a. There is data incompatibility and command incompatibility among stand alone software. With integrated software, there is command and data compatibility.

2. _____ combines several common applications to make a single program.
   - a. The all-in-one packagec.
   - b. The integrated series
   - A systems integrator
   - d. Utility software

---

a. The all-in-one package is the most widely known and used integrated software. It combines several applications in one program.

3. The _____ enables the user to move data residing in memory from one stand-alone package to another.
   - a. The all-in-one packagec.
   - b. The integrated series
   - A systems integrator
   - d. Utility software

---

c. Topview from IBM is an example of a systems integrator which allows the user to move data residing in memory form one stand-alone package to another.

4. _____ is an example of a lower-end integrated package that is frequently used in homes and schools
   - a. Enable software
   - b. Framework
   - c. Symphony
   - d. Microsoft Works

---

d. Microsoft Works by Microsoft Corporation is an affordable program that is often used in homes and schools.

5. The _____ feature allows the user to enlarge the current window so that it fills up the entire screen while the other windows temporarily disappear.
   a. windows
   b. utility
   c. zoom
   d. systems integrator

---

c. If too many windows are open at the same time, working in the current window can be difficult. The zoom feature allows the user to zoom in on the current window to make it easier to work in it.

❏ TRUE/FALSE

T F   1. Integrated packages never became as popular as originally predicted.
T F   2. For data to be compatible, programs must use the same data format.
T F   3. The functions found in an all-in-one package as just as complete as the functions offered in single application programs.
T F   4. Of the four types of integrated software, utility software offers the best integration capabilities.
T F   5. The current trend in software development towards compatibility is one reason why sales of integrated software is decreasing.

❏ MATCHING

   a. stand-alone software
   b. systems integrator
   c. utility software
   d. integrated series
   e. multimedia computing

1. Separate application programs that share a common command set are called _____.

2. _____ include calculators, calendars, telephone dialers, and notepads that are loaded into RAM.

3. A single application program that serves one purpose is called _____.

4. The _____ makes it possible to move data residing in memory from one program to another.

5. _____ integrates color video images, sound, and computer applications.

1. List the applications most often included in an integrated software package.

2. Why are integrated programs rarely used in homes?

3. What are some reasons why integrated packages never became as popular as originally predicted?

4. What are the three standards to which integrated software must conform?

5. Describe some uses of multimedia computing.

Expert Systems

❑ KEY TERMS

Artificial intelligence Field of research currently developing techniques whereby computers can be used to solve problems that appear to require imagination, intuition, or intelligence.

Consultation When a user accesses information from an expert system.

Domain In expert systems technology, the domain is the area of activity or specialty that the system includes, such as medicine, law, or tax analysis.

Domain knowledge The knowledge pertaining to a specific domain that is gathered from outside sources.

Expert systems technology The development of computer software that simulates human problem-solving abilities. An expert system uses human knowledge that has been collected and stored in a computer to solve problems that ordinarily can be solved only by a human expert.

Heuristics The rules and trial-an-error methods that expert systems programs use to solve problems.

Inference engine The "brain" of an expert system that allows the computer to make inferences from data stored in its knowledge base.

Knowledge base In expert systems technology, the knowledge base contains everything necessary for understanding, formulating, and solving problems.

❑ SUMMARY

Expert systems technology is a subfield of research in the area of artificial intelligence. Expert systems technology is the development of computer software that simulates human problem-solving abilities. An expert system sues human knowledge that has been collected and stored in a computer to solve problems that ordinarily can be solved only by a human expert.

A consultation is when an end user accesses information from an expert system. The first step in developing an expert system is to gather information about the domain, which is the field or area of activity. The domain knowledge is the knowledge pertaining to a specific domain. The knowledge base is made up of the domain knowledge and special heuristics, or rules of thumb and trial-and-error methods that experts use to solve problems. Most expert systems are rule based.

The "brain" of an expert system is the inference engine, which is the component where the reasoning is performed. The inference engine includes procedures regarding problem solving.

Features of expert systems include an explanation capacity, a user interface that is user friendly, an explanation subsystem, forward chaining, backward chaining, and fuzzy sets.

Two recent trends in expert systems are to apply them to real-time problems and to combine expert systems with neural networks. Real-time expert systems handle data that is changing rapidly.

❏ STRUCTURED LEARNING

1. In expert systems, the _____ contains everything necessary for understanding, formulating, and solving the problem.
   a. domain knowledge
   b. consultation
   c. knowledge base
   d. heuristics

---

c. The knowledge base is made up of the domain knowledge and special heuristics.

2. The "brain" of an expert system is the _____.
   a. domain knowledge
   b. inference engine
   c. knowledge base
   d. heuristics

---

b. The inference engine is the component where the reasoning is performed. It includes procedures regarding problem solving.

3. The people who typically perform consultations on an expert system are _____.
   a. the designers of the system
   b. end users
   c. knowledge engineers
   d. artificial intelligence specialists

---

b. The people who use expert systems, the end users typically have little or no knowledge of artificial intelligence.

4. A(n) _____ is the ability of an expert system to trace the conclusion drawn back to the reasons what that conclusion was reached.

    a. explanation capacity
           c. backward chaining

    b. forward chaining
           d. conclusion capacity

a. The explanation capacity allows the expert system to explain its advice or recommendations by showing the specific rules that were applied to reach the end conclusion.

5. _____ is the art and science of building an expert system.

    a. Artificial intelligence
           c. Expert systems technology

    b. Knowledge engineering
           d. Inference engineering

b. The growth in expert systems technology led to the development of a new discipline called knowledge engineering, which is the art and science of building an expert system.

❏ TRUE/FALSE

T F   1. An expert system shell is an expert system that is available as an application software package and contains the inference engine, user interface, and the commands of an expert system.

T F   2. No expert systems have been developed for home use.

T F   3. A current trend in expert systems technology is to connect expert systems to Lisp machines.

T F   4. The knowledge base is the component where the reasoning takes place in an expert system.

T F   5. Expert systems technology is one outcome of research in artificial intelligence.

❏ MATCHING

    a. forward chaining
           d. heuristics

    b. backward chaining
           e. real-time

    c. fuzzy sets

1. Expert systems use _____ to provide probalistic definitions to knowledge.

2. The rules of thumb and trial-and-error methods that experts use to solve problems are called _____.

3. A search technique that applies user-specific knowledge to the knowledge-base rules is called _____.

4. Complex _____ computer systems control a large number of functions at a very fast rate.

5. Applying a user-goal to the appropriate rules in the expert system in order to determine if a solution exists is called _____.

1. What problem in the business sector has it been predicted that expert systems will help to solve?

2. List the four methods for connecting expert systems with neural networks.

3. List the type of tasks expert systems are currently being used to perform.

4. What is an expert system shell?

5. Explain how a real-time expert system is used.

Graphical User Interface and Windows 3.0

❏ KEY TERMS

Clipboard The intermediary place where data from one file is temporarily placed before it is integrated into another file.

Command-line user interface A user interface that, by design, requires the user to type in commands that are then executed by the computer's operating system.

Graphical-user interface A user interface to the computer's operating system that uses graphics, or pictures, and menus to simplify the user's task of working with the computer.

Icon A graphic, or picture, used to represent such things as an application, document, folder, or disk on a graphical user interface.

Multitasking Running two or more programs on a computer at once.

Window The portion of the screen that holds a specific file or application.

❏ SUMMARY

Graphical User Interface, or GUI, incorporates four elements: windows, icons, menus, and a pointing device. A GUI uses a mouse to point to icons representing documents and programs. The command menus are pull-down or pop-up and separate windows can be displayed on the screen at the same time.

Computers either have a GUI, or a CLI, which stands for command line interface. With CLI, commands are mostly typed at the keyboard, a mouse in not needed, there are no icons, and applications do not run in a window. The central part of Windows is the Program Manager. Any installed DOS of Windows-based program can be started from the Program Manager. The File Manager performs many file management operations such as moving files or searching for files. The Control Panel allows the user to modify Windows to suit his or her needs. Windows also comes with many accessories such as a notepad, a clock, a calendar, a daily appointment book, a cardfile, a calculator, Paintbrush, Write, and Terminal.

Features found in Windows include standard mode memory management, 386 enhanced mode, multi-tasking, dynamic data exchange, and the help feature. The minimum hardware requirements for Windows 3.0 are a PC with 640K of memory and a CGA or better color screen or a Hercules monochrome screen.

1. Computers with a _____ interface do not need a mouse, commands are typed at the keyboard, do not use icons, and do not run applications in windows.
   - a. command line
   - b. graphical user
   - c. user friendly
   - d. PC compatible

---

a. IBM PCs and IBM clones that do not use a GUI program use CLI, or command line interface.

2. In Windows, the _____ allows the user to modify the program to suit his or her needs.
   - a. Program Manager
   - b. File Manager
   - c. Control Panel
   - d. Terminal

---

c. The Control Panel allows the user to set the options for screen colors, fonts, and printers.

3. _____ is a way of using hard-disk space to simulate RAM.
   - a. Standard mode memory
   - b. Virtual memory
   - c. dynamic data exchange
   - d. Multitasking

---

b. With virtual memory Windows 3.0 can perform as if it had access to many times as much RAM as is actually available.

4. _____ is a method by which programs operating under Windows can swap various types of data.
   - a. Standard mode memory
   - b. Virtual memory
   - c. dynamic data exchange
   - d. Multitasking

---

c. Any Windows-based program that supports dynamic data exchange can exchange data with any other Windows-based program supporting DDE.

5. _____ is the ability to run or more application at the same time.
   - a. Dynamic data exchange
   - b. The virtual machine
   - c. Windowing
   - d. Multitasking

---

d. The 386 enhanced mode allows the user to multitask operations. In the enhanced mode, six or more applications can be open at the same time, with each application running in its own window.

❏ TRUE/FALSE

T F   1. The IBM PC was the first computer to utilize GUI.
T F   2. The applications that will run under Windows are limited.
T F   3. In order to use standard mode memory management, the computer must have an 80286 or 80386 microprocessor and at least 1MB of RAM.
T F   4. The central part of Windows is the Program Manager.
T F   5. The future of Windows partially depends on the development of OS/2's Presentation Manager.

❏ MATCHING

a. clipboard

b. icon

c. virtual memory

d. File Manager

e. DDE

1. A method by which programs operating under Widows can exchange data with one another.

2. _____ is a way of using hard-disk space to simulate RAM.

3. The intermediary place where data from one file is temporarily placed before it is integrated into another file is called the _____.

4. A graphic used to represent such things as an application, document, folder, or disk on a graphical user interface is called a(n) _____.

5. The _____ displays a tree-oriented view of disks in multiple windows.

❏ SHORT ANSWER

1. What does the statement "all applications running under Windows have a standard user interface" mean?

2. What does the statement "Windows 3.0 eliminates the 640K barrier for DOS" mean?

3. List some GUIs other than Windows.

4. What are the three major part of Windows?

5. What are the four elements of GUI?

BASIC SUPPLEMENT, SECTION I

Introduction to BASIC

❏ STRUCTURED LEARNING

1. Which of the following is true of BASIC?
    a. BASIC is unpopular because it is difficult to learn.
    b. BASIC is short for Beginner's All-purpose Symbolic Instruction Code.
    c. BASIC is a programming language that has no syntax rules.
    d. BASIC was developed in the mid-1950s.

---

b. BASIC is a programming language developed in the mid-1960s. It is popular because it is an easy-to-learn general purpose language, and it does contain rules for spelling, syntax, grammar, and punctuation.

2. The first step of the programming process is _____.
    a. designing the program
    b. writing the program
    c. compiling, debugging, and testing the program
    d. defining the problem

---

d. The first step of the programming process is defining the problem. Then the solution can be designed and the program written, compiled, debugged, and tested.

3. The flowchart symbol for a processing step is _____.
    a. ⬭   c. ▢
    b. ▱   d. ◇

---

c. ▢ is used for an input or output step; ⬭ shows where the program starts or stops; ◇ is used to show where a decision is to be made.

4. The series of steps necessary to achieve the desired output from the available input is the _____.
   a. structure chart
   b. syntax
   c. algorithm
   d. documentation

---

a. Structure charts are used to break the problem into more manageable subparts, syntax refers to the grammar and punctuation of the programming language; documentation explains the program to humans; an algorithm specifies all the necessary steps in the problem solution.

5. _____ are used by the programmer to communicate with the operating system of the computer.
   a. BASIC statements
   b. ANSI commands
   c. BASIC commands
   d. SYS commands

---

c. BASIC commands enable the programmer to communicate with the operating system to perform functions such as saving and loading programs.

❏ WORKSHEET

1. Write a flowchart for a program to calculate the cost of materials for building a bookcase. The expenses are as follows:
   a. Lumber $14.25
   b. Nails $2.04
   c. Paint $5.00
   d. Sandpaper $1.90

Add a 6% sales tax to the total amount. The total cost should then be output.

2. Write the pseudocode for the problem in Question 2.

3. Develop a structure chart for the task of building a bookcase.

4. Write the BASIC commands to perform the following tasks.
   a. Prepare the computer to have a new program entered.
   b. Load a program named "PROG1.BAS" from disk into the computer's main memory.
   c. Save a program named "BILL" on disk.
   d. Execute a program that is currently in main memory.

5. State the BASIC commands to perform the following tasks.
   a. Display a program in main memory on the terminal screen.
   b. Display lines 150-200 of a program in main memory on the screen.
   c. Display line 20 of a program in main memory on the screen.

BASIC Fundamentals

❏ STRUCTURED LEARNING

1. Which of the following is not true of line numbers?
   a. They must be positive integer values.
   b. Lines numbers specify the order of execution of BASIC statements.
   c. Line numbers must be in increments of 1.
   d. Line numbers can be used as labels to refer to specific statements in a program.

---

c.   Line numbers can follow any size increment as long as they are positive integers between 1 and the upper limit of the system being used. Line numbers are used both as labels and to indicate the order of execution of BASIC statements.

2. Constants ____.
   a. are values that do not change during program execution
   b. must be numeric values
   c. change their values throughout the program's execution
   d. are the same as variables

---

a.   Constants may be numeric or character string values that do not change during the execution of a program. Variables, on the other hand, are storage locations the values of which can change during program execution.

3. Which of the following is true of exponential notation?
   a. It is never used with very large or small numbers.
   b. The "E" represents the power to which 10 is raised.
   c. The signed number following the "E" is the mantissa.
   d. A plus sign (+) indicates the decimal point is to be shifted to the right.

---

d.   The plus sign (+) indicates the decimal point is to be shifted right the specified number of places and the minus sign (-) indicates it is to be shifted left.

4. Which of the following is not a valid numeric variable name?
   a. X1
   c. Q4
   b. ZENITH
   d. 9J

---

d. A numeric variable name can be either one letter alone or one letter followed by letters or digits.

5. Which of the following is a valid string variable name?
   a. FULL$
   c. $ZILL
   b. $6
   d. 7$

---

a. FULL$. A string variable name consists of a letter followed by letters or digits and ending with a dollar sign ($).

❑ WORKSHEET

1. Which of the following constants are invalid? If they are invalid, indicate why.
   a. 100.9
   d. 9,701
   b. "Valentine's Day"
   e. -480
   c. 'Christmas'

2. Write the following assignment statements.
   a. Assign the value 16 to a variable named NMR.
   b. Assign the character string "Boston University" to a variable named U$.
   c. Assign your name to a variable named NM$.
   d. Assign your age to a variable named AG.

3. Identify the invalid variable names. Tell why they are invalid and change them to make them valid.
   a. 8$
   d. F 7
   b. $X
   e. QUIZ$
   c. F

4. What is the purpose of using variables and variable names?

5. What is the result of the following mathematical expressions?
   a. $T * (2 + 3) / S \wedge 3$ where $T = 8$ and $S = 2$
   b. $C * D / 2 \wedge 4 * 9$ where $C = 6$ and $D = 8$
   c. $X + Y * (Z / 4 + 6)$ where $X = 4$, $Y = 3$, and $Z = 20$

6. Write a BASIC statement to assign the result of the following equations to a variable.

a. $\dfrac{5+6}{(9*25)}$

b. $\dfrac{7*2^3}{{}^B\!/_C}$

c. $\dfrac{Z^9\,(.5)}{(Z+X)/2}$

d. $\dfrac{\frac{3}{4}+2}{X+3\,(\frac{1}{2})}$

7. Which of the following LET statements are invalid? Why?

a. 20 LET S = "TRACEY MILLER"

b. 30 LET 3.895 = X

c. 40 LET Z$ = "JANUARY"

Auto Parts, Inc. sells spark plugs, gaskets, and batteries. On the average, 12 percent of the spark plugs, 10 percent of the gaskets, and 7.5 percent of the batteries are defective. Auto Parts has just completed inventory. There are 7,500 spark plugs, 10,000 gaskets, and 300 batteries on hand.

The purchasing agent of Auto Parts wants a report listing the part, the approximate number of good parts, the approximate number of defective parts, and the total number of each part on hand.

The output should appear as follows:

```
PART            GOOD            DEFECTIVE       TOTAL
_____

XXXXXXXX        #####           ######          ######
    .               .               .               .
    .               .               .               .
    .               .               .               .
```

You have been asked by the Way-Sales Computer Company to determine the highest selling computer during its annual Computer Bargain Sale. Following is a list of the computers, the number on hand at the beginning of the sale, and the number on hand after the sale:

COMPUTER	BEGINNING	END
Apple IIGS	35	15
Apple IIe	15	5
Apple Macintosh SE	50	9
IBM-PS/2	30	11
Compaq	25	15

Write a program to compute the percentage sold for each computer during the sale. Use the following output:

```
COMPUTER        PERCENTAGE

XXXXXXXXXXX       XX
         .         .
         .         .
         .         .
```

Input and Output

❏ STRUCTURED LEARNING

1. Which of the following is not true of the READ statement?
   a. The READ statement should be used with a prompt.
   b. The READ statement is used in conjunction with the DATA statement.
   c. READ statements are useful when large amounts of unchanging data need to be entered to a program.
   d. READ statements are located in a program wherever the logic of the program indicates the need for data.

---

a. READ statements are useful when reading large quantities of unfrequently changing data. The data is placed in DATA statements. However, because the READ statement is not interactive, no prompt is used.

2. Which of the following would be a correct response to the following INPUT statement?

```
30 INPUT "ENTER BOOK'S NAME, PRICE, AND QUANTITY ON HAND";TTLE$,PR,Q
```

    a. `CATCH-22 5.95 14`   c. `"CATCH-22","5.95","14"`
    b. `CATCH-22,5.95,14`   d. `CATCH-22;5.95;14`

---

b. Each variable in an INPUT statement must have a value entered to it. The values must be separated by commas and must match the type of variable.

3. What will be output by the following?

```
100 PRINT "COMPUTERS","ARE";"PEOPLE","TOO"
```

    a. `COMPUTERS        AREPEOPLE        TOO`
    b. `COMPUTERS        ARE              PEOPLE          TOO`
    c. `COMPUTERSAREPEOPLE                               TOO`
    d. `COMPUTERSAREPEOPLETOO`

---

a. A comma causes the next output to be in the next print zone whereas a semicolon causes it to be in the next column.

4. Which of the following PRINT statements is invalid?
   a. 10 PRINT "AGE IS ",21   c. 20 PRINT HAPPY BIRTHDAY
   b. 20 PRINT "JANUARY NINTH"   d. 30 PRINT 10 + 14

---

c. PRINT statements can contain variables, character strings, numeric literals, or arithmetic expressions. However, all character strings must be enclosed in quotation marks.

5. Use a _____ statement when you want the user to enter data during program execution; use a statement when you want the data to be contained within the program itself.
   a. PRINT, DATA   c. READ, INPUT
   b. DATA, PRINT   d. INPUT, READ

---

d. INPUT statements allow the user to enter data during execution. When the READ statement is used, DATA statements contain the input.

❑ WORKSHEET

1. What is output by the following statement?
   PRINT USING "\   \ $ ##.#";"OWED",13.36

2. What advantage does the INPUT statement have over the READ/DATA statements when entering data?

3. What advantage does the READ/DATA statement have over the INPUT statement when reading data?

4. What values will be assigned to the variables in the following READ statements?
   ```
   10 READ X, Y
   20 READ Z$,A
   30 DATA 9
   40 DATA 10, JASON, -393
   ```

5. Which of the following PRINT statements contain errors? Correct those errors.
   a. 10 PRINT "NAME" "I.D. NUMBER" "OCCUPATION"
   b. 20 PRINT X:Y:Z$
   c. 30 PRINT "DARREN",,"ASTRE";
   d. 40 PRINT "THE DATE IS;D$
   e. 50 PRINT TAB(10); "LICENSE NUMBER"
   f. 60 PRINT A;B;C,

6. Which of the following program segments will give the same output?

a.
```
10  READ W,X,Y,Z
20  S = W + X + Y + Z
30  PRINT S
40  DATA 9,10,-3,2,0
```

c.
```
10  READ W,X,Y,Z
20  READ Y
30  PRINT W + X + Y + Z
40  DATA 9,10
50  DATA  -3,2,0
```

b.
```
10  READ W,X
20  READ Y,Z
30  PRINT W + X + Y + Z
40  DATA 9,10,-3,2,0
50  DATA 9,10
60  DATA -3,2
```

d.
```
10  READ W,X,Y
20  READ Z
30  S = W + X + Y + Z
40  PRINT S
```

7. The following values must be stored in different variables. Show three different ways that this can be accomplished.

CHAIRS, 8, TABLES, 2

8. What will happen when this program segment is executed?
```
40  READ PL$
50  READ PPL
60  READ PL$,PPL
70  DATA "CHEROKEE",4000,"BIG TIMBER"
80  DATA "8,000"
```

Jim and Bob have decided to stop smoking and would like to know how much money they will save per week and per year. Bob smokes one and one-half packs a day at $2.05 a pack, and Jim smokes one-half pack a day at $2.20 a pack. Format your output like that shown below:

```
SMOKER'S        NO. PACKS      COST           AMT. SAVED      AMT. SAVED
NAME            PER DAY        PER PACK       PER WEEK        PER YEAR
--------        ---------      --------       ----------      ----------

XXXXX             XX            X.XX           XX.XX            XXXX.X
```

❏ PROGRAMMING PROBLEM 2

The Census Bureau has asked you to write a program that will print a report consisting of the name of the household and the number of people residing in the house. At the end of the report, the Census Bureau wants a total of the number of people included in the report. The output should look as follows:

```
NAME            # RESIDENTS

XXXXXXXXXXXX    ##
XXXXXXXXXXXX    ##
XXXXXXXXXXXX    ##
XXXXXXXXXXXX    ##
TOTAL:          ###
```

Use READ/DATA statements to enter the input for the report shown below:

```
NAME            # RESIDENTS

Douglas         4
Morgan          8
Owens           11
Sergisson       2
```

The Decision Statement and Functions

❏ STRUCTURED LEARNING

1. Which of the following is not an example of a control statement?
   - a. IF/THEN
   - b. GOTO
   - c. END
   - d. IF/THEN/ELSE

---

c. The END statement merely stops program execution. The IF/THEN, IF/THEN/ELSE, and GOTO statements all allow the programmer to control the order in which program statements are executed.

2. Which of the following causes an unconditional transfer of control?
   - a. IF/THEN
   - b. PRINT
   - c. IF/THEN/ELSE
   - d. GOTO

---

d. The GOTO statement always transfers control to the stated line whereas the IF statement only transfers control if certain conditions are met. The PRINT statement never causes a transfer of control.

3. Which of the following statements assigns 3 to R?
   - a. `10 R = SGN(2 + 1)`
   - b. `10 R = ABS(-3)`
   - c. `10 R = SQR(3)`
   - d. `10 R = COS(3)`

---

b. The absolute value of -3 is 3 whereas part (a) assigns a value of 1 to R, part (c) assigns the square root of 3 to R, and part (d) assigns the cosine of 3 to R.

4. The general format of the statement which allows a programmer to define his or her own functions is
_____.
   - a. line# DEFINE function name(argument) = expression
   - b. line# DEF function name(argument) = expression
   - c. line# USERDEF function name = expression
   - d. line# function name(DEF) = expression

---

b. The statement used to define a function is DEF.

5. What value is assigned to T$ by the following instructions?

```
10 T$ = MID$("419-555-448",5,3)
```

    a. 555   c. 448

    b. 9-5   d. 555-4

---

a. The MID$ function returns the character string starting at the position indicated by the first integer and continuing for the number of characters specified by the second integer.

❑ WORKSHEET

1. Correct any of the following IF/THEN statements that are invalid.

    a. `10 IF N$ = "LAST" THAN 99`

    b. `20 IF X  2 PRINT X`

    c. `100 IF X = J THEN 10`

2. What flowchart symbol is used to represent an IF statement?

3. Draw a flowchart to represent the following program segment.

```
30 INPUT "ENTER YOUR AGE";AG
40 IF AGE = 21 THEN PRINT "ADULT" ELSE PRINT "MINOR"
```

4. Why is it preferrable to use IF statements rather than GOTO statements whenever possible?

5. Given the following flowchart, write the corresponding program segment.

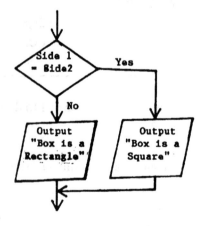

6. What value will be returned by each of the following numeric functions?
   a. ABS(143)
   b. SQR(100)
   c. SGN(83)

7. Write a program segment that prompts the user to enter a character string and then prints the number of characters in that string.

8. Which of the following will print the five left-most characters of the string stored in A$?
   a. 10 PRINT LEFT$(A$,5)   c. 30 PRINT LEFT$(A$,1,5)
   b. 20 PRINT LEFT$(5,A$)   d. 40 PRINT LEFT$(A,5,A$)

9. What is the purpose of the VAL function?

10. What function performs the opposite of the VAL function?

A shoe store has devised a system to help detect errors in recording inventory. The last two digits of every stock number must be the sum of the preceding three digits. For example, the stock number QB412.07 is valid because 07 is the sum of 4 + 1 + 2. Write a program that reads a stock number and prints a message stating whether the stock number is valid. Use the following data to test your program.

QB371.11
UT491.14
UT307.11
AT478.19
QB115.08
QA919.17
QB497.20
UT410.05
AT731.11

❑ PROGRAMMING PROBLEM 2

An income tax agent is checking wage earners in the income bracket $20,000 to $30,000. Write a program that will allow the user to enter the amount of a wage earner's income and the amount of taxes paid. If taxes paid are below 27.5 percent of gross earnings, compute the additional amount due and print a stern message to the wage earner, specifying the amount due. If the amount due is over $5,000.00, add a penalty charge of 1.5 percent to the amount due. Print an error message if the income is below $20,000 or above $30,000.

Earnings	Tax Paid
23,000	6279.00
34,000	9282.00
30,000	8000.00
28,540	2791.42

Looping

❑ STRUCTURED LEARNING

1. The FOR/NEXT loop is used _____.
   a. for counting loops
   b. for loops that are controlled by a trailer value
   c. in situations in which it is not known how many times the loop will need to be executed when it is first entered
   d. for transferring control to the end of a program

---

a. FOR/NEXT loops are used for counting loops in which the exact number of repetitions is known when the loop is first entered.

2. In the following FOR statement, 5 is the _____.

```
10 FOR I = 20 TO 5 STEP -2
```

   a. initial value
   b. terminal value
   c. loop control variable
   d. step value

---

b. 5 is the terminal value. When I (the loop control variable) is less than 5, the loop will terminate.

3. What will be the output of the following program segment?

```
10 LET N$ = "MARY"
20 FOR I = 1 TO 4
30    PRT$ = LEFT$(N$,I)
40    PRINT PRT$,
50 NEXT I
```

   a. MARY   MARY   MARY   MARY
   b. MARY   MAR   MA   M
   c. M   MA   MAR   MARY
   d. Y   RY   ARY   MARY

---

c. Each time this loop is executed, the character string that is printed will be increased by one until the entire string is output.

4. What will be output by the following program segment?

```
10 N$ = "MARY"
20 CNT = 1
30 WHILE CNT <= LEN("MARY")
40     PRINT CNT,
50     CNT = CNT + 1
60 NEXT
```

a.	1	2	3	4	5
b.	M	MA	MAR	MARY	
c.	1	2	3	4	
d.	MARY	MARY	MARY	MARY	

---

c. The value of CNT starts at 1 and is incremented by 1 until 4 (the length of MARY) is reached.

5. On the microcomputers, the end of the WHILE loop is marked by a(n) _____ statement whereas on the VAX, it is marked by a(n) _____ statement.

   a. END, STOP   c. NEXT, WEND
   b. STOP, END   d. WEND, NEXT

---

d. IBM and Macintosh Microsoft and the Apple indicate the end of a WHILE loop by using a WEND statement whereas on the VAX, the end is indicated by the NEXT statement.

❑ WORKSHEET

1. Give the value of each of the following where X = 2 and Y = 3.

```
110 FOR K = (Y * 8) TO (2 ^ Y) STEP -X
```

   a. initial value =
   b. terminal value =
   c. step value =
   d. loop control variable (2nd time through the loop) =

2. Using a FOR/NEXT statement, write a program segment to print the multiples of 5 from 100 down through 75.

3. What will be the output of the following program segments?

   (X = 9; Y = 4)

   a. 10 FOR I = (X - 8) TO 18 STEP Y
      20   PRINT I,
      30 NEXT I

   b. 100 FOR Z = X TO -Y STEP -3
      110   PRINT Z;Z + 1
      120 NEXT Z

   c. 50 FOR J = X TO X - 1
      60   PRINT J
      70 NEXT J

4. Correct the following FOR/NEXT loops.

   a. 10 FOR I = 10 TO 1 STEP -1
      .
      .
      .
      50 NEXT

   b. 20 FOR J = 2 TO 12 STEP 2
      30   S = S + J
      40   GOTO 20
      50 NEXT J

   c. 50 FOR K = 1 TO 10 STEP 2
      60   K = K + 1
      70   PRINT K
      80 NEXT K

   d. 10 FOR X = 1 TO 10 STEP 1
      20   PRINT X
      30   S = X + 2
      40 NEXT I

5. Which of the following will print the average price of six books?

   a. 10 S = 0
      20 FOR I = 1 TO 6
      30   READ P
      40   S = S + P
      50 NEXT I
      60 A = S / 6
      70 PRINT A
      80 DATA 5.95, 3.23, 4.97
      90 DATA 10.29, 20.30, 32.97
      99 END

   b. 10 FOR I = 1 TO 6
      20   S = 0
      30   READ P
      40   S = S + P
      50 NEXT I
      60 PRINT S / 6
      70 DATA 5.95, 3.23, 4.97
      80 DATA 10.29,20.30,32.97
      99 END

6. Correct the following program segment.

```
a. 10 FOR I = 1 TO 10
   20     FOR J = 2 TO 4
   30         IF (I + J) = 6 THEN 20
   40         PRINT I,J
   50     NEXT I
   60 NEXT J
```

7. How many times will the statement PRINT I,J be executed in each of the following program segments?

```
a. 10 FOR I = 15 TO 3 STEP -3     b. 10 FOR I = -8 TO 0 STEP 4
   20     FOR J = 1 TO 3             20     FOR J = 1 TO 5 STEP 2
   30         PRINT I,J              30         FOR K = -2 TO 5 STEP 2
   40     NEXT J                     40             PRINT I,J
   50 NEXT I                         50         NEXT K
                                     60     NEXT J
                                     70 NEXT I
```

8. Give an example of a situation in which it would be appropriate to use a WHILE loop. Give an example of a situation in which a FOR loop would be most appropriate.

9. Rewrite the following program segment using a WHILE loop instead of a FOR/NEXT loop.

```
10 ITM = 6
20 WHILE ITM >= 1
30     READ T$,Q
40     ITM = ITM - 1
50 NEXT
60 DATA "HAMMER",24,"PLIERS",12
70 DATA "CHISEL",8,"DRILL",18
80 DATA "WRENCH",20,"SCREW DRIVER",42
```

10. What will be the output from the following program?

```
10 FOR N = 1 TO 2
20     FOR I = 1 TO 3
30         FOR J = 8 TO 10 STEP 2
40             PRINT N;I;J,
50         NEXT J
60         PRINT
70     NEXT I
80 NEXT N
99 END
```

❏ PROGRAMMING PROBLEM

The trustees of Bowling Green High School are considering a measure to give the ten full-time teachers a 4 percent, 4.5 percent, or 5 percent pay raise. To make their decision, they want to know how much additional money they would need in each of the three cases. Write a program to show sample salaries of $12,000 to $18,000 (by $1,000) and the three proposed increased salaries for each. Create a table like the following:

SALARY	+4%	+4.5%	+5%
12,000	12480	12540	12600
13,000	13520	13585	13650
.	.	.	.
.	.	.	.
.	.	.	.

❏ PROGRAMMING PROBLEM 2

Modify the program for Problem 1 so that an extra line of summary information is included at the bottom of the chart. This line should give the total of the seven sample salaries and the totals of each of the three increased salary columns. Also, print the difference between the sample salary total and each of the three increased totals. A sample summary follows:

```
         .              .              .              .
         .              .              .              .
         .              .              .              .
   18,000         XXXXXX         XXXXX         XXXXXX
   XXXXXX         XXXXXX         XXXXX         XXXXXX


+4% gross difference = XXXXX
+4.5% gross difference = XXXXXX
+5% gross difference = XXXXX
```

BASIC SUPPLEMENT, SECTION VI

Modularizing Programs

❏ STRUCTURED LEARNING

1. A sequence of instructions following the main portion of a program that may be executed as many times as necessary, but typed only once, is called a _____.
   - a. subfunction
   - b. procedure
   - c. routine
   - d. subroutine

---

d. In BASIC, subroutines are subprograms, usually placed after the main program, that can be executed as often as necessary.

2. The GOSUB statement _____.
   - a. is used to transfer the flow of control from the main body of the program to a subroutine
   - b. is a conditional transfer statement
   - c. is used to transfer the flow of control from a subroutine to the main body of the program
   - d. may appear only once in a program

---

a. The GOSUB statement unconditionally transfer the flow of control from the main body of the program to a subroutine.

3. The RETURN statement is _____.
   - a. used to transfer the flow of control from the main body of the program to a subroutine
   - b. a conditional transfer statement
   - c. used to transfer the flow of control from a subroutine to the calling program
   - d. optional in a subroutine

---

c. The RETURN statement is always required to transfer control from the end of the subroutine back to the calling program.

4. When a subroutine is _____, control is transferred to it.
   - a. written
   - b. called
   - c. implemented
   - d. transferred

a. When control is transferred to a subroutine through the use of the GOSUB or ON/GOSUB statements, it is said to be called.

5. In a driver program, the main body of the program consists mainly of _____.
   a. IF statements
   b. calls to subroutines
   c. INPUT, READ, and PRINT statements
   d. nested FOR/NEXT loops

---

b. The primary purpose of a driver program is to call subroutines; the subroutines then perform the processing.

❑ WORKSHEET

1. What determines where control will be transferred when using an ON/GOSUB statement?

2. To what line will control be transferred when the following program segment is executed?
   ```
   50 A = 14 / 7 + 2
   60 ON A GOSUB 3000,4000,5000,6000
   ```

3. Why is this program segment invalid?
   ```
   100 VOWEL$ = "E"
   110 ON VOWEL$ GOSUB 2000
   ```

4. What programming principle does the following subroutine violate?
   ```
   3000 REM *** SUBROUTINE TO CALCULATE OVERTIME PAY ***
   3010 IF HRS <= 40 THEN RETURN
   3020 PAY = PAY + (HRS - 40) * PAY * 0.5
   3030 RETURN
   ```

5. What is wrong with the following segment?
   ```
   10 GOSUB 1000
   20 PRINT X
      .
      .
      .
   1000 REM ***        SUBROUTINE        ***
   1010 REM
   1020 X = 12 * 77
   9999 END
   ```

6. Where will program control be transferred if the following statements are executed?

```
260 X = 4 + 23
270 N = X / 8 + 1
280 ON N GOSUB 1000,2000,3000,4000
```

7. Rewrite the following program segment using a single ON/GOSUB statement.

```
350 IF X = 6 THEN GOSUB 9000
360 IF X = 9 THEN GOSUB 2000
370 IF X = 12 THEN GOSUB 3000
```

8. Why is it good programming practice to divide a program into subroutines?

9. Write a subroutine that checks a user-supplied value for the variable ACCTNUM and prompts the user to reenter the value if it is not in the range of 1-999.

10. What is wrong with the following program segment?

```
240 INPUT "ENTER AMOUNT OF FINE";FINE
250 IF FINE  20.00 THEN GOSUB 1000 ELSE GOSUB 1040
260 GOSUB 2000
     .
     .
     .
1000 REM *** PRINT FINE ***
1010 REM
1020 PRINT "A PENALTY OF 15% HAS BEEN ADDED TO YOUR FINE"
1030 FINE = FINE + (FINE * 0.15)
1040 PRINT \ PRINT "YOU OWE $";FINE
1050 RETURN
```

The public library needs a program to calculate the total cost of the books it adds to its collection. This cost includes not only the purchase price of the book but also the cost of processing the book. Processing costs are dependent upon two factors: (1) the type of the book (reference, circulating, or paperback) and, (2) whether or not the book is a duplicate of one already in the library. It is cheaper to process books that are duplicates of those already in the library's collection. Processing costs are as follows:

Reference Book

Not a duplicate	$8.50
Duplicate	$7.40

Circulating Book

Not a duplicate	$7.82
Duplicate	$6.60

Paperback

Not a duplicate	$4.60
Duplicate	$3.10

Stewart and Sons Jewelers need a program to accept its salespersons' sales for each of four months. Output the total sales and average sales for each person, and total sales for all four months. Use READ/DATA statements to allow the following data to be entered:

Stu Birch	7,457.90	5,071.63	4,921.16	5,717.05
Monica Bulas	1,125.16	927.19	1,674.84	1,970.15
Carol Carson	2,257.08	3,716.84	2,116.93	1,877.45
David Toth	871.69	1,199.72	1,299.60	941.38
Irene Drake	4,412.77	2,128.91	3,008.97	2,364.33
Anne Ling	2,740.08	3,165.75	2,981.39	1,866.40
XXX	0	0	0	0

The output should look similar to this:

```
SALESPERSON              TOTAL        AVERAGE
XXXXXXXXXXXXX            XXXXX        XXXX
         .                  .            .
         .                  .            .
         .                  .            .


TOTAL SALES = $XXXXXXX
```

Arrays

❏ STRUCTURED LEARNING

1. A(n) _____ is a group of storage locations in memory in which data elements can be stored.
   - a. DIM
   - b. subscript
   - c. array
   - d. section

---

c. An array is a group of storage locations in memory. The elements stored in the array are related to one another and the entire array is given a single name.

2. Subscripts _____.
   - a. are used to indicate individual elements in an array.
   - b. can be negative
   - c. may not be mathematical expressions
   - d. are used to indicate the address in memory of a simple variable

---

a. Subscripts are used to reference individual elements of an array and can be expressions, variables, or integers that evaluate as numeric values.

3. References to specific elements of arrays are called _____.
   - a. unsubscripted variables
   - b. subscripted variables
   - c. array variables
   - d. element variables

---

b. Using a subscript with a variable name allows a specific array element to be accessed.

4. An array with rows and columns is called a _____.
   - a. one-dimensional array
   - b. two-dimensional array
   - c. big array
   - d. list

---

b. A two-dimensional array is an array with rows and columns.

5. The programmer can specify the number of elements an array can contain using a _____.
   a. DCL statement (short for declare)
   b. DIM statement (short for dimension)
   c. SPEC statement (short for specification)
   d. RES statement (short for reserve)

---

b. Compilers will automatically reserve space for ten or eleven elements in an array. If an array is to contain more than ten or eleven elements, the number of elements for which space must be reserved is specified in a DIM (short for dimension) statement.

❑ WORKSHEET

1. What will be the values of the following given these arrays and simple variables?

Array X	Array Z	
50	1	I = 1
100	2	J = 3
25	30	K = 4
125	16	

   a. X(K)
   b. Z(K - J)
   c. X(I) + X(J)

   d. Z(I + 3)
   e. Z(2) - Z(I)
   f. X(J - I)

2. What will be the values in array A after the following program segment is executed?
```
100 FOR J = 10 TO 1 STEP -2
110     READ A(J)
120 NEXT J
130 DATA 10,2,9,5,12
140 DATA 20,22,98,73,7
```

3. Write a BASIC statement to reserve storage locations for an array named N that will contain 99 elements.

4. What will be the output from the following program?
```
100 FOR I = 1 TO 6
110     READ X(I)
120 NEXT I
130 FOR J = 1 TO 6 STEP 3
140     PRINT X(J), X(J + 1), X(J + 2)
150 NEXT J
160 DATA 9,8,7,6,5,4
170 END
```

5. How many storage locations are reserved for the array R by the following statement (do not count the zero positions)?

```
30 DIM R(20,10)
```

6. Given this array and variables, what will be the value of the following?

Array T

55	105	205	$I = 1$
475	155	395	$J = 2$
385	995	765	$K = 4$

    a. T(I,J)   d. T(J,K - J)

    b. T(J,I)   e. T(J,J)

    c. T(K - I,I)   f. T(I,I + J)

7. What will be the output of the following program?

```
80   DIM X(3,4)
90      FOR I = 1 TO 3
100        FOR J = 1 TO 4
110           READ X(I,J)
120           PRINT X(I,J),
130        NEXT J
140        PRINT
150     NEXT I
160 DATA 7,9,22,1,36,5
170 DATA 11,6,12,32,10,49
180 END
```

8. Write a program that will read the values below into a two-dimensional array and print the total of the elements in the second column.

1	3	9
12	15	18
21	24	27
30	33	36

9. Write a program segment that will total the rows of the array G with the dimensions (3,5), and place those totals in another array R.

10. Write a program segment to total all the elements of the following array:

```
30 DIM W(4,3)
```

❑ PROGRAMMING PROBLEM 1

There are four grocery stores in town: Kathy's Supermarket, Key Food, Church's, and The Market Place. The local consumer group has decided to do some testing of the prices of foods at the various stores. The consumer group has asked you to write a program to determine which store has the best bargains on hamburger, lettuce, and bread. Write a program that prints a report of the various prices at the stores and also prints the store that has the best food buys. The prices are listed below:

	Hamburger	Lettuce	Bread
Kathy's Supermarket	1.08/lb	0.99/head	0.35/loaf
Key Food	1.11/lb	0.89/head	0.40/loaf
Church's	0.99/lb	0.99/head	0.45/loaf
The Market Place	1.18/lb	0.89/head	0.38/loaf

The University newspaper is planning to print a comic section with their paper. The editor of the paper has asked you to print a list of the comic strips in alphabetical order. The comic strips to be printed are as follows:

PEANUTS
HEATHCLIFF
HERMAN
DENNIS THE MENACE
DICK TRACY
FAMILY CIRCUS
MARY WORTH
LI'L ABNER
SUPERMAN
BEETLE BAILEY
HAGAR THE HORRIBLE
THE WIZARD OF ID
BRENDA STARR
B.C.
SPIDERMAN

ANSWER KEY TO STUDY GUIDE

Chapter 1
Introduction to Information Processing

❑ TRUE/FALSE

1. F	3. F	5. T	7. F	9. F
2. T	4. T	6. F	8. T	10. T

❑ MATCHING

1. a	3. f	5. g	7. j	9. c
2. i	4. e	6. d	8. b	10. h

❑ SHORT ANSWER

1. Input, processing, output

2. Analog computers measure changes in continuous physical or electrical states, such as pressures, temperature, or voltage. Digital computers count data. Data is represented by discrete "on" and "off" (conducting/nonconducting) states of the computer's electronic circuity.

3. Arithmetic operations; logical comparisons of relationships between values; storage and retrieval operations.

4. Supercomputers are the largest, fastest, and most expensive computers. Their chips require liquid coolant to prevent melting. They are used for lengthy, complex problems.

5. Computer-based training (CBT) is popular for teaching job skills in business and industry and subject matter at schools. Multimedia is popular in schools and combines text, audio and video, and graphics to create an integrated educational system.

6. The three steps in data output are retrieving data from storage for use by the decision maker, converting data into a form that humans can understand and use, and communicating—that is, providing information to the proper users at the proper time and in the proper form.

7. The central processing unit handles processing. This includes the circuitry for arithmetic and logical operations and primary memory.

8. Today the market for minicomputers is weakening because the increased capacities and improved software of microcomputers has led to the increase use of micros in the traditional minicomputer market. Many companies are linking microcomputers with existing mainframes or minicomputers instead of buying new minicomputers.

9. Information processing is all of the steps involved in converting data into information, and thus includes data processing as well as the process of converting data into information.

10. Feedback is the process of evaluating output and making adjustments to the input or the processing steps. This ensures that the processing continues to result in good information.

Chapter 2
The Evolution of Computers

❏ TRUE/FALSE

1. F	3. T	5. T	7. T	9. T
2. F	4. F	6. T	8. F	10. F

❏ MATCHING

1. g	3. b	5. i	7. c	9. d
2. e	4. h	6. f	8. a	10. j

❏ SHORT ANSWER

1. Heat. Vacuum tubes needed air conditioning, yet one tube failed about every 15 minutes. Supercomputer chips generate too much heat unless they are submerged in a special liquid coolant bath.

2. Tax officials needed faster, more accurate methods of computing taxes because tax systems began expanding. Businesses became more complicated, too.

3. The concepts introduced in Jacquard's loom were that information could be coded on punched cards; cards could be linked in a series of instructions; and such programs could automate jobs.

4. Four parts in Babbage's ideas for an analytical engine that are similar to parts used in today's computers are a mill for calculating; store for holding instructions and intermediate and final results; an operator or system for carrying out instructions; and a device for "reading" and "writing" data on punched cards.

5. Remote terminals are computer terminals located away from a main computer and linked to it through cables such as telephone lines.

6. Some ideas that will indicate a fifth generation of computers are that artificial intelligence will imitate human thought and people will communicate with their computers by speaking in their native languages.

7. They enabled programmers to use more English-like ways of writing programs rather than using machine language, which was tedious and often error-prone.

8. The TRS-80 was available in a store, so that the customer could just walk into a retail store and buy a low-priced personal computer. The IBM PC quickly became the standard in small business computers.

9. Besides selling equipment, most hardware manufacturers provide support services in the form of education, training, and maintenance and repair.

10. Early software was rarely free of "bugs" or errors. The software industry lagged behind advances in hardware technology. Old programs had to be rewritten for new machines and skilled programmers were scarce.

Chapter 3
Introduction to Information Systems

❏ TRUE/FALSE

1. T	3. T	5. F	7. F	9. F
2. F	4. F	6. F	8. T	10. T

❏ MATCHING

1. j	3. f	5. b	7. i	9. h
2. d	4. g	6. e	8. a	10. c

❏ SHORT ANSWER

1. To be meaningful information must be timely, relevant, accurate, verifiable, complete, and clear.

2. Information frequently loses its value as it ages. Therefore, information usually must be current to be useful. For some decisions, however, the information may include figures that span a five-year

period so timely information is not always current information. Timely information is appropriate information that is available when needed.

3. Three ways to verify information are as follows:
   a. Compare the new information with other information that is accurate.
   b. Rekey the data and compare it with the original.
   c. Conduct an audit trail back to its source.

4. Survival is the primary goal of a system. Feedback helps in this goal by pinpointing the system's strengths and weaknesses.

5. Information is data that has been processed and made useful for decision making. The components of an information system are hardware, software, data, and people.

6. Most professional organizations encourage high standards and keep members up to date on innovations and developments in their fields.

7. A maintenance programmer continually changes and revises programs. This programmer needs extensive programming experience and a high level of analytical ability.

8. People bring the parts of an information system together and coordinate all activities within the system. Their roles are as providers, users, and clients.

9. Inventory control regulates the quantity of raw materials available. Scheduling of facilities helps eliminate wasted machine time and scheduling conflicts. Engineering systems assist in designing and testing new products.

10. A computerized inventory system is often used in conjunction with order processing. By combining the two, orders can be filled more quickly, accurately, and efficiently.

Chapter 4
Hardware

❏ TRUE/FALSE

1. F	3. F	5. F	7. F	9. F
2. F	4. T	6. F	8. T	10. T

❏ MATCHING

1. c	3. h	5. i	7. d	9. b
2. f	4. a	6. e	8. j	10. g

❏ SHORT ANSWER

1. The three parts of the CPU are the control unit, the arithmetic/logic unit, and memory.

2. Logical comparisons include equal to, not equal to, greater than, less than, equal to or greater than, and equal to or less than.

3. Semiconductor memory is composed of circuitry on silicon chips. The chips are designed to store data in locations called bit cells, which are capable of being either on or off. The bit cells are arranged in matrices.

4. Both read-only and nondestructive read memory can be read repeatedly, but the nondestructive read can be changed if the program instructs the computer to do so. Read-only memory is hard-wired and can only be changed by rewiring.

5. The 16 characters used in the hexadecimal number system are the digits 0 through 9 and the letters A through F.

6. 1   1   0   0   1   0   0   1

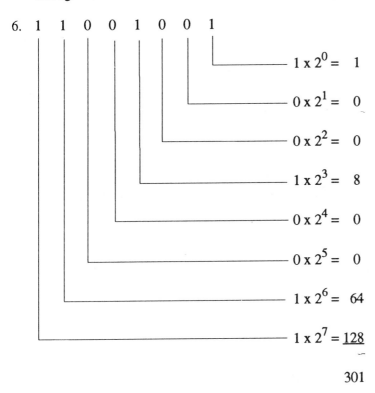

$$1 \times 2^0 = 1$$
$$0 \times 2^1 = 0$$
$$0 \times 2^2 = 0$$
$$1 \times 2^3 = 8$$
$$0 \times 2^4 = 0$$
$$0 \times 2^5 = 0$$
$$1 \times 2^6 = 64$$
$$1 \times 2^7 = \underline{128}$$

301

7.
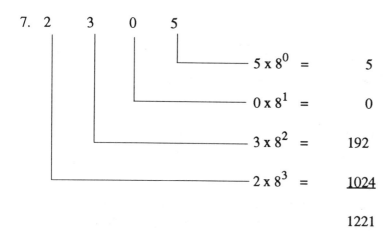

5×8^0	=	5
0×8^1	=	0
3×8^2	=	192
2×8^3	=	<u>1024</u>
		1221

8. Coding schemes include the following:
   - four-bit binary coded decimal (BCD)
   - six-bit BCD
   - eight-bit Extended Binary Coded Decimal Interchange Code (EBCDIC)
   - American Standard Code for Information Interchange (ASCII)
   - ASCII-8

9. The two parts of the instruction code are the op code and the operand. The operation code (op code) indicates to the control unit what function is to be performed. The operand indicates the primary storage location of the data on which to operate.

10. Bit cells are arranged in matrices often 8 rows by 8 columns. Electrical current is sent through the wires. An "on" state is where the electronically charged wires intersect; all others are "off."

Chapter 5
Input and Output

❑ TRUE/FALSE

1. T	3. T	5. T	7. T	9. F
2. F	4. T	6. T	8. T	10. T

❑ MATCHING

1. f	3. h	5. i	7. j	9. g
2. c	4. e	6. b	8. d	10. a

1. Although both rely on reflected light to translate data to machine form, optical-character readers can detect shapes such as characters, but optical-mark readers can only detect the position of marks.

2. Nonimpact printers may have special paper requirements, occasional poor type-image quality, and are unable to make carbon copies. The cartridges of ink or toner also may be expensive.

3. Key-to-magnetic data entry involves keying (or typing) data at a keyboard, after which the data is saved onto magnetic storage media such as tapes or disks.

4. Data entry has traditionally involved recopying data that has already been typed or written onto paper documents. The process can involved many errors in transcription.

5. The Universal Product Code (UPC) is a type of bar code consisting of sets of vertical bars that identify the manufacturers of items. The code is read by a wand reader or a scanner, and matched with data already in the computer; thus, data entry occurs directly from the product—that is, the source—rather than being keyed in by a cash register attendant who could make mistakes in keying.

6. Impact printers print characters by mechanically striking the paper; nonimpact use heat, laser, or photographic techniques.

7. Dot-matrix printers have a print element that contains pins arranged in a rectangular matrix. Only the pins that are needed to help form a particular character are activated at each strike.

8. Nonimpact printers include the electrostatic, electrothermal, ink-jet, laser, and xerographic.

9. Visual display terminals produce output faster and quieter than printers. They are useful when hard copy output is not necessary. Also, they permit the user to see the output almost instantly, thus are appropriate for inquiry-and-response applications.

10. The POS terminal often has a keyboard for optional data entry, a panel to display the price and other information, a cash drawer, and a printer that provides the cash receipt.

Chapter 6
Storage Devices

□ TRUE/FALSE

1. F	3. T	5. T	7. T	9. T
2. T	4. F	6. T	8. F	10. T

❏ MATCHING

1. i	3. f	5. e	7. d	9. j
2. h	4. b	6. a	8. g	10. c

❏ SHORT ANSWER

1. Density means how closely packed the data is. On magnetic tape, densities of 1,600 characters per inch are common and some tapes can store up to 6,250 characters per inch. On an optical disk, a single line one inch long can store about 5,000 pits or bits of data.

2. Backup copies are copies of the original, made to protect a company against data loss due to sabotage, natural disasters, environmental problems such as a water pipe break, or \accidents.

3. A cylinder describes the way the access arms hold the read/write heads over the same track on each disk in the disk pack. The arms may move the heads to the second track or the tenth track, but all move at once to that track. Since the tracks are concentric, the invisible shape that is suggested is the cylinder.

4. Advantages of magnetic disks are as follows:
   - Files can be organized sequentially or for direct-access processing.
   - Fast access allows files to be accessed or changed immediately.
   - Quick response can be made to inquiries.
   - One transaction can change several files at once.

5. A cartridge tape is a high-density tape that requires 90 percent less space than magnetic tape.

6. A mass storage system for minicomputers uses small floppy disks.

7. CCDs are made of silicon similar to semiconductor memory and are 100 times faster than bubble memory, but slower than semiconductor RAM.

8. Data recorded with a helium-neon laser cannot be erased once it has been written, thus, it is safe from tampering accidental or otherwise. The laser actually puts a hole in the tellerium film.

9. Storage is necessary because the amount of data required by a program or set of instructions usually exceeds the capacity of memory.

10. Floppy disks come in two sizes, 5 1/4 inches (with a flexible plastic jacket and exposed read/write notch) and 3 1/2 inches (with a hard plastic jacket and a metal slide that opens to expose the disk). The actual disks are made of plastic and coated with a magnetizable oxide substance.

Chapter 7
File Organization and Data Base Design

❏ TRUE/FALSE

1.	T	3.	F	5.	T	7.	F	9.	T
2.	T	4.	F	6.	F	8.	F	10.	T

❏ MATCHING

1.	c	3.	f	5.	g	7.	j	9.	h
2.	i	4.	e	6.	b	8.	a	10.	d

❏ SHORT ANSWER

1. A DBMS is a set of programs that serves as the interface between the data base and the programmer, operating system, and users.

2. Three file designs are sequential, indexed-sequential, and direct-access.

3. Three advantages of data bases are as follows:
    - Data redundancy is minimized.
    - Data can be stored in a manner that is useful for a variety of applications.
    - Updating involves only one copy of the data.

4. Activity refers to the proportion of records processed during an updating run. Volatility refers to the frequency of changes to a file during a given time period.

5. Two advantages of sequential processing are as follows:
    - File design is simple.
    - It can be cost effective when at least half the records in a master file are updated.

6. In the relational data structure, the data elements are placed in a table with rows and columns. Each data element has a unique location in the table and is referred to by its rows and column numbers, called subscripts.

7. A simple data structure is a sequential arrangement of data records whose fields are called attributes. If the records are in a specific sequence, the list is called a linear structure.

8. Advantages of direct-access processing and file design include the following:
    - Master files need not be sorted.
    - Only master records to be updated are accessed.
    - Access to a record only takes a fraction of a second.
    - Several files can be updated at the same time.
    - Flexibility in handling inquiries.

9. An inverted structure contains indexes for selected attributes in a file. The addresses of records having these attributes are also listed so that records can then be referenced by the addresses.

10. Advantages of indexed-sequential processing include the following:
- Files are well suited for both inquiries and large processing run
- Access time to specific records is faster than sequential file organization.

Chapter 8
Microcomputers

❏ TRUE/FALSE

1. T	3. F	5. T	7. T	9. T
2. T	4. T	6. F	8. F	10. F

❏ MATCHING

1. g	3. i	5. h	7. f	9. c
2. j	4. b	6. a	8. e	10. d

❏ SHORT ANSWER

1. Slots are positions on the motherboard in which to place add-on cards that can expand the capabilities of a microcomputer. You must open the microcomputer case to install a card. A port is an outlet on the outside of the computer in which you can plug a cable to a printer or mouse.

2. Microprocessors are commonly used in microwave ovens, calculators, typewriters, sewing machines, vending machines, traffic lights, gas pumps, and cars.

3. The working directory is the directory the user is currently in.

4. Three major groups of microcomputers include portables, desktops, and supermicrocomputers. A portable is a major group, but is also one of the computers in that group. It weighs between 12 and 17 pounds and runs on battery power. It has a hard disk and floppy diskette drive. The transportable is one of the computers in the portable category. It does, however, need an external power supply. It weighs more than 17 pounds.

5. Three types of portable computers are laptop, notebook, and transportable machines. (A fourth is the portable.)

6. Laptops are technologically sophisticated due to the microprocessors that give them the power of full-size computers, the flat display panels that make them slim and easy to carry, and the battery power that frees them from an external power source.

7. Booting means that a small program in ROM starts loading the operating system from either a hard disk or floppy disk into the computer when the computer is turned on.

8. A transparent operating system is one that lessens the amount of knowledge required by the user of the microcomputer. Most use icons and pull-down menus that are controlled by moving a mouse.

9. Compatibility is the ability to use one manufacturer's equipment or software with another's. A coprocessor can make a computer compatible with another operating system and allow software compatible with that other operating system to be run on the computer.

10. Word processing, electronic spreadsheet, data-management, and graphic software are the basic business software packages.

Chapter 9
Telecommunication and Networks

❏ TRUE/FALSE

1. T	3. F	5. T	7. T	9. T
2. F	4. T	6. T	8. T	10. T

❏ MATCHING

1. g	3. d	5. c	7. j	9. f
2. i	4. a	6. h	8. e	10. b

❏ SHORT ANSWER

1. The three types of modems are the acoustic coupler, direct connect, and internal.

2. The term **modem** is derived from the terms **mod**ulation and **dem**odulation.

3. A concentrator can accept data from only one device at a time. A multiplexor can handle more than one I/O device at a time.

4. Some of the most common communication channels include telephone lines, coaxial cable, fiber optic cable, and microwave channels.

5. The three grade classifications of channels are narrow bandwidth, voice-grade, and broad-band.

6. The three transmission modes of channels are as follows:
   - Simplex—unidirectional or one-way transmission
   - Half duplex—data flows in two directions but only one way at a time
   - Full duplex—data flows in both directions simultaneously

7. The assumption being made is that not all terminals will be ready to send or receive data at a given time.

8. The two most frequent uses of communications processors are message switching and front-end processing.

9. Three advantages of time sharing are that it is an economical means for small users to access a large system; each user seems to possess a private computer; and it provides a greater number of application programs at a lower cost.

10. Some of the more common network configurations include star, ring, hierarchical, bus, and fully distributed configurations.

Chapter 10
System Software

❏ TRUE/FALSE

1.	F	3.	T	5.	T	7.	T	9.	T
2.	F	4.	T	6.	T	8.	F	10.	F

❏ MATCHING

1.	g	3.	b	5.	a	7.	e	9.	c
2.	d	4.	i	6.	h	8.	j	10.	f

❏ SHORT ANSWER

1. The interrupts occur in operating systems that handle both batch and online jobs. If a device such as a workstation, printer, or storage device sends a message to the CPU to do a job, normal processing is suspended (the CPU is interrupted) so that the CPU may direct the operation of the I/O device.

2. The operating system contains control programs and processing programs.

3. The job-control program translates the job-control statements written by a programmer into machine language instructions that can be executed by the computer.

4. Multiprogramming requires that programs in memory must be kept separate. This is accomplished using regions or partitions and keeping the programs in the correct region or partition is known as memory management or memory protection.

5. Virtual memory is used to overcome limited space problems in multiprogramming.

6. Only the immediately needed portion of a program must be in memory at any given time. The rest of the program and data can be kept in storage.

7. It offers more flexibility because these people do not have to think about how they are going to fit their programs into memory. Moreover, the use of memory is optimized.

8. In segmentation, each program is broken into variable-sized blocks called segments; each is a logical part of the program. The operating system allocates memory according to the size of these logical segments. In paging, memory is divided into physical areas of fixed size called page frames. They are all the same size. The programs are broken into equal sizes called pages. One page can fit into one page frame of memory.

9. One limitation of virtual memory is that it requires extensive online storage. Another limitation is that the operating system is highly sophisticated and requires significant amounts of memory.

10. A front-end processor is a small CPU serving as an interface between a large CPU and peripheral devices. A back-end processor is a small CPU that serves as an interface between a large CPU and a large data base stored on direct-access storage devices.

Chapter 11
Software Development

❏ TRUE/FALSE

1. F	3. F	5. T	7. T	9. T
2. T	4. F	6. F	8. T	10. T

❏ MATCHING

1. d	3. j	5. c	7. e	9. i
2. g	4. a	6. h	8. f	10. b

1. The following are the four steps in the software development process:
   (1) Define and document the problem.
   (2) Design and document a solution.
   (3) Write and document the program.
   (4) Debug and test the program and revise the documentation.

2. The loop enables the program to alter the normal next-sequential-instruction process and go back to a previous statement, so that a sequence of statements can be performed as many times as needed.

3. Some of the problems of early programming include these:
   - productivity was low
   - programs were not reliable
   - programs could not always handle invalid data
   - programs were not easy to maintain

4. Action diagrams are complete enough that the common mixing of different types of charts and pseudocodes is not needed. They also lend themselves to top-down design.

5. The two broad categories of structured programming techniques are structured design techniques and structured coding. Structured design techniques are those characteristics that affect the manner in which the program solution is designed. Structured coding techniques are those characteristics that affect the style in which actual program is written.

6. Some advantages of top-down design are as follows:
   - It prevents the programmer from being overwhelmed by the size of the job.
   - It discovers early whether a specific solution will work.
   - Each box on the structure chart can be written as a separate module.

7. In the informal design review, the system design documentation is studied before the actual coding of program modules takes place. The formal design review is used after the detailed parts of the system have been sufficiently documented. A formal design review may be held to discuss the overall completeness, accuracy, and quality of the design.

8. The system analyst is trained to examine an existing system, analyze data about it, define goals clearly, and so on, but a programmer is trained to use a particular programming language to write a program. The programmer may know little about business or information needs or corporate constraints.

9. Some programming statements common to most high-level languages include comments, declarations, input/output statements, computations, comparisons, and loops.

10. A dump lists the contents of memory locations, usually in hexadecimal form. If an incorrect value is found, it can be used to help locate an error in programming. The trace, on the other hand, lists

the steps followed during program execution in the order in which they occurred. Using a trace, the programmer can determine where the program logic failed to do what was expected.

Chapter 12
Programming Languages

❏ TRUE/FALSE

1. T	3. F	5. F	7. T	9. T
2. F	4. F	6. T	8. F	10. T

❏ MATCHING

1. c	3. h	5. f	7. g	9. i
	e	6. a	8. d	10. b

❏ SHC

1. A low-level language is oriented toward the hardware, and high-level language is oriented toward the programmer.

2. Structured languages allow programmers to easily divide programs into modules, each performing a specific task. These languages provide a wide variety of control structures for using selection and loop logic patterns.

3. A procedure-oriented language puts the emphasis on describing the computational and logic procedures required to solve a problem. A problem-oriented language is one in which the problem and solution are described without the necessary procedures being specified. Problem-oriented languages require little programming skill.

4. General-purpose languages can be used to solve a wide variety of programming problems. Special-purpose languages are for specific uses such as educational, business, or scientific jobs.

5. Answers will vary, but the main advantage of assembly language is that it can be used to develop programs that use memory space and processing time efficiently.

6. What equipment or software changes are planned for the future? Does the company have requirements for using a specific language?

7. BASIC stands for Beginner's All-Purpose Symbolic Instruction Code. COBOL stands for COmmon Business Oriented Language.

8. The query language portion requires the user to construct English-like statements to extract and manipulate data in the data base. The report generator enables a user to design the format of reports that are created from data in the data base. The application generator gives the user a simplified method of developing an application program.

9. Logo enables students to see what they are doing through the use of a triangular object called a turtle, which leaves a graphic trail in its path. While manipulating the turtle, students learn structured programming techniques that are transferrable to other structured languages such as Pascal.

10. Ada was developed by the Department of Defense, which realized that no current high-level language could meet its needs.

Chapter 13
Application Software

❑ TRUE/FALSE

1. T	3. T	5. F	7. T	9. F
2. T	4. T	6. T	8. T	10. F

❑ MATCHING

1. c	3. j	5. e	7. g	9. i
2. h	4. f	6. b	8. a	10. d

❑ SHORT ANSWER

1. The following are three advantages of commercial software:
   - They can contain more features than software developed in-house.
   - The reliability can be assumed.
   - The vendors usually offer good quality support for the user.

2. Three broad categories of commercial software packages are these:
   - productivity tools
   - functional tools
   - end-user development tools

3. Productivity tools include these types of software:
   - word processors
   - graphics packages
   - spreadsheets
   - file managers

4. Graphics packages can be used in a variety of ways to develop presentation graphics, including pie charts, bar charts, and line graphs. Cameras can be used to take slides from the screen displays.

5. Examples of functional tools include accounting, manufacturing, sales, marketing, and desktop publishing packages.

6. A tool for the horizontal market is designed for general use and is not customized. A tool for the vertical market has a very specific market and can be tailored to meet the needs of that market.

7. One advantage of a simulation package is that after it has shown that using the model in simulation consistently yields correct results, it is no longer necessary to check the results against reality.

8. Some specific uses of expert systems are as follows:
   ■ diagnosis of infectious diseases
   ■ estate planning
   ■ location of mineral deposits
   ■ long-range business planning

9. Expert systems only cover very small fields of knowledge; decision support systems attempt to allow managers to make decisions based on a wide range of data and options.

10. In evaluating software, DATAMATION considers these factors:
   ■ performance
   ■ operations
   ■ I/O functionality
   ■ vendor support

Chapter 14
System Analysis and Design

❏ TRUE/FALSE

1.	T	3.	F	5.	F	7.	F	9.	F
2.	F	4.	T	6.	T	8.	T	10.	T

❏ MATCHING

1.	h	3.	b	5.	e	7.	a	9.	j
2.	d	4.	i	6.	g	8.	c	10.	f

1. The first step in system analysis is to formulate a statement of overall objectives—the goals of the system. Identifying these objectives is essential to the identification of the information that the system will require.

2. Reasons for conducting system analysis include solving a problem, responding to new requirements, implementing new technology, and making broad system improvements.

3. Four internal sources of data gathering are interviews, system flowcharts, questionnaires, and formal reports.

4. Three ways to analyze data are grid charts, system flowcharts, and decision logic tables.

5. A system analysis report is a report presented to management after the system analysis. The report explains the present system and all the alternatives, along with the constraints, scope, costs, and resources required to develop a new system.

6. In system analysis, the focus is on what the old system does and should be doing. In system design, the focus is on how a new system can be developed to meet information requirements.

7. Some of the constraints in any organization include limitations on financial budgets, personnel, computer facilities, and time.

8. Some changes, as a result of new laws or regulations, may be required without regard to economic benefits.

9. The three classifications are system documentation, program documentation, and procedure documentation.

10. Parallel conversion, pilot conversion, phased conversion, and crash (direct) conversion are four approaches to system conversion.

Chapter 15
Management Information Systems and Decision Support Systems

❏ **TRUE/FALSE**

1. T	3. F	5. T	7. T	9. F
2. T	4. T	6. F	8. T	10. T

❑ MATCHING

1. d	3. b	5. a	7. c	9. i
2. f	4. h	6. j	8. e	10. g

❑ SHORT ANSWER

1. The goal of an MIS is to get the correct information to the appropriate manager at the right time and in a useful form.

2. The activities at the top level of management include establishing goals and determining strategies to achieve the goals. The decisions are strategic and the activities are future-oriented and involve a great deal of uncertainty.

3. The function of lower-level management is controlling company results—keeping the results in line with plans and taking corrective actions if necessary.

4. Problems at the top level are nonrepetitive, have great impact on the organization, and involve a great deal of uncertainty; therefore, it is difficult to design MIS for top-level management.

5. Predictive reports are those used for planning. They are based on decision models in which a manager can manipulate variables to get response to "what if" kinds of queries. These reports are suited to the tactical and strategic decisions that middle-level and top-level managers make.

6. People who have unrealistic expectations for an MIS may not have been involved in the analysis, design, and programming, and do not understand the system limitations.

7. They apply to organizing a company's activities, because they are the basic organizational structures. The development of an MIS is an integrated approach to organizing a company's activities.

8. MIS supports only structured or operation decisions, whereas a DSS supports unstructured or strategic decisions.

9. Some obstacles to decision-support systems include management resistance, lack of management sophistication, and interdepartmental communication problems.

10. Each manager must have a decision model based on his/her perception of the system.

Chapter 16
The Impact of Computers on People and Organizations

❏ TRUE/FALSE

1. F	3. F	5. T	7. T	9. F
2. T	4. T	6. F	8. T	10. T

❏ MATCHING

1. d	3. j	5. h	7. i	9. b
2. c	4. a	6. f	8. e	10. g

❏ SHORT ANSWER

1. Older people may not accept computers favorably. In addition, many people are afraid that if they make a mistake, valuable information will be lost. Another common fear is the fear of losing a job to computers. Depersonalization is another fear.

2. Factors determining the extent of job displacement due to technology are these: the goals that are sought from the use of the computers; the growth rate of the organization; the planning that has gone into the acquisition and use of the computer.

3. People would be more comfortable about using jargon, would know how a computer deals with data and how it can be saved from loss, and would be more comfortable with technology.

4. Electronic mail, teleconferencing, and telecomputing are forms of electronic office communication.

5. Computer conferencing involves entering data, usually at a keyboard, at a computer terminal and placing it in the system for other people to read. The readers can read the messages at their own convenience and send a return. Audio conferencing involves three or more parties in what is basically a conference call. All parties must be present and all parties talk.

6. Ergonomics in computer fields involves the study of designing hardware and software to increase employee productivity and comfort. This is becoming increasingly important to workers who may suffer fatigue, eyestrain, and stress from working with equipment that is not of ergonomically sound design.

7. The domino effect works like this: If one business improves its operations through the use of computers, other businesses must also computerize to remain competitive.

8. CAD allows an engineer to design, draft, and analyze a prospective product using computer graphics on a video terminal. Its partner, CAM, enables engineers to design and analyze the manufacturing process to make this product.

9. Computers analyze the data obtained by the X rays, high-frequency sound waves, or laser beams. Powerful new data-processing capabilities have made it possible for workers to determine the difference between serious flaws and minor flaws.

10. Students will suggest other answers, but here are some factors: The keyboard should have a comfortable slant and layout, and should be adjustable or portable. Lighting should be placed so that there is little glare on the VDT, or else there should be a glare shield on the monitor. Printers should be put in another room, so that the workstation is in a quiet location.

Chapter 17
Computer Security, Crime, Ethics, and the Law

❏ TRUE/FALSE

1. T	3. T	5. F	7. T	9. F
2. T	4. F	6. F	8. T	10. F

❏ MATCHING

1. f	3. i	5. e	7. c	9. g
2. b	4. j	6. h	8. a	10. d

❏ SHORT ANSWER

1. A computer crime is a criminal act that poses a greater threat to a computer user than it would a noncomputer user, or a criminal act that is accomplished through the use of a computer.

2. Computer crime includes sabotage, theft of services, property crimes, and financial crimes.

3. Fire, natural disaster, environmental problems, and sabotage are hazards to a computer system.

4. Decryption is the process of translating data that is in secret code back into plain text.

5. The Privacy Act of 1974 contains these provisions:
   - Individuals should be able to find out what information about themselves is being recorded and how it will be used.
   - Individuals should be able to correct wrong information.
   - Information collected for one purpose should not be used for another purpose without the consent of the individual involved.
   - Organizations creating, manipulating, using, or divulging personal information must ensure that the information is reliable and must take precautions to prevent misuse of the information.

6. The Uniform Commercial Code is a set of provisions proposed by legal experts to promote uniformity among the state courts. Common law is based on customs and past judicial decisions in similar cases. The UCC is a better system of protection for the buyer. It abolishes the concept of caveat emptor.

7. The UCC applies to computer transactions when the contract is for goods, not services.

8. Express warranties are created when the seller makes any promise or statement of fact concerning the goods being sold which the purchaser uses as a basis for purchasing the goods. The seller warrants, or guarantees, the goods will meet the purchaser's needs.

9. An implied warranty of merchantability exists if the seller is considered a merchant. The warranty guarantees that the good purchased will function properly for a reasonable period of time.

10. An implied warranty of fitness requires that the purchaser communicate to the supplier the specific purpose for which the product will be used. The purchaser then relies on the supplier to select suitable merchandise.

Chapter 18
Computers in Our Lives: Today and Tomorrow

❑ TRUE/FALSE

1. F	3. F	5. T	7. T	9. T
2. T	4. T	6. F	8. F	10. T

❑ MATCHING

1. b	3. d	5. i	7. j	9. g
2. f	4. h	6. a	8. e	10. c

1. The two problems of placing electronic components close together are excessive heat and cross talk.

2. Gallium arsenide chips resist radiation.

3. Fiber optics offers the advantages of speed and accuracy in data transmission. They will be able to carry a number of signals such as those for high-definition television, which normal telephone lines cannot carry.

4. Artificial intelligence is based on human intelligence, which in itself is not clearly understood. New computers and languages only begin to imitate human intelligence at higher levels.

5. Electrocardiograms, X rays, blood, vision and hearing testing, blood pressure, height and weight measurement are all part of multiphasic health testing.

6. Because they do not require surgery, CAT scans and NMR can prevent possible infections, blood clots, and fatigue associated with surgery. Tests can be conducted without invading the body.

7. Voice recognition systems can recognize a number of voices using a small vocabulary, or can recognize the large vocabulary of one speaker. The systems require the speaker to talk in distinct syllables. Research is focusing on systems that accept larger vocabularies from more speakers who talk in continuous, or flowing, speech.

8. Microprocessors can be used to control the movements of artificial limbs and can be used to control pacemakers.

9. There are several types of CAI software. Drills quiz students; tutorials introduce new materials, simulations imitate real-world situations; games teach new concepts; problem solving software encourages exploration and application of previous knowledge. Multimedia lets students create presentations that show what they have learned.

10. In 1958, Jack Kilby of Texas Instruments introduced the first integrated circuit. Subtract 1958 from the current year to arrive at the number of years ago this occurred.

Section I
Word Processors

❏ TRUE/FALSE

1. F   2. F   3. T   4. T   5. F

❏ MATCHING

1. b   2. c   3. d   4. e   5. b

❏ SHORT ANSWER

1. A page-oriented word processor treats a text file as a series of pages, very much like a typewriter. Text is broken up into pages and only one page of a document can be created or saved on disk at a time. In addition, only one page of a document can be edited at a time. A document-oriented word processor treats a document as a single continuous file. The entire document can be saved with one command. Pages do not have to be worked on separately in a document-oriented word processor since the bottom of one page and the top portion of the next page appear on the screen at the same time.

2. The status line supplies format information about the document such as the line and column number where the cursor is located, the page number of the text on the screen, and the number of words or characters in the document.

3. The three print-formatting processes are page design, paragraph layout and character attributes.

4. The typical block operations are:
    ■ Block-delete
    ■ Block-move
    ■ Block-copy
    ■ Block save
    ■ Block-merge

5. The five categories of word processors are:
   - personal
   - professional
   - corporate
   - legal
   - desktop publishing

Section II
Spreadsheets

❏ TRUE/FALSE

1. T   2. F   3. T   4. F   5. T

❏ MATCHING

1. e   2. b   3. c   4. a   5. d

❏ SHORT ANSWER

1. The term "what if" questions refers to questions seeking to find out what will happen to certain numbers in a spreadsheet if other numbers change.

2. A range of cells can be printed, copied, moved, or deleted.

3. The common categories of functions are statistical, mathematical, financial, string, and logical.

4. Macros can be used to automate frequently used spreadsheet commands, typing the same label repeatedly in a spreadsheet, performing a repetitive procedure requiring a series of sequential commands such as printing a spreadsheet, and developing a customized worksheet for someone who is not familiar with spreadsheet programs.

5. "Add-in" products work in conjunction with an existing spreadsheet program to enhance it. Examples of add-in products include word processing, sideways printing programs, add-in graphics, add-in data base managers, and add-in communications.

Section III
Data Managers

❑ **TRUE/FALSE**

1. F   2. T   3. F   4. T   5. F

❑ **MATCHING**

1. c   2. d   3. b   4.   5.

❑ **SHORT ANSWER**

1. Most data managers can add or delete data within a file, search a file for certain data, update or change data in a file, sort data into some order, print all or part of the data in a file.

2. The main difference between a flat-file manager and a relational data base is that a relational data base can draw from more than one file at a time.

3. Pharmacies use data bases to store drug and patient information to help pharmacists avoid giving patients medicines that may be harmful. Data managers are used to create mailing lists. They can then be used with word processors to produce personalized form letters for organizations or individuals on the mailing list.

4. With indexing, a list can be ordered by more than one key without holding redundant data. An index consists of only a list of keys in order and a pointer to the master list.

5. The two classifications of programming languages are procedural and nonprocedural. A nonprocedural language allows the user to tell the program *what* is to be done. A procedural language requires the youse to tell the computer *how* to do it. Non procedural languages are easier to use.

Section IV
Integrated Software

❑ **TRUE/FALSE**

1. T   2. T   3. F   4. F   5. T

❑ MATCHING

1. d   2. c   3. a   4. b   5. e

❑ SHORT ANSWER

1. Data managers, spreadsheet analysis, word processing, and graphics are the applications often included in an integrated software package.

2. Integrated software is rarely used in homes because the price of these programs can range from $300 to $1500. In addition, sophisticated integrated programs often require more memory than the typical home computer has.

3. No application is an integrated package is quite as good as the best available stand-alone of that application. All users do not want or need all the functions that come in an integrated package. Add-in products allow users to choose exactly what they want rather than just having to take everything that comes in an integrated package. Sand-alone programs are becoming increasingly compatible.

4. The three standards to which integrated software must conform are:
    ■ The software consists of application programs that are usually separate.
    ■ The software provides easy movement of data among the separate applications.
    ■ A common group of commands is used for all the applications in the software package.

5. A laser-disk encyclopedia that included voices, video, and sound to expand upon the text and drawings would be an example of multimedia computing. Multimedia computing is currently being used for industrial training, education,a nd public information kiosks.

Section V
Expert Systems

❑ TRUE/FALSE

1. T   2. F   3. F   4. F   5. T

❑ MATCHING

1. c   2. d   3. a   4. e   5. b

❑ SHORT ANSWER

1. Expert systems are seen as possibly solving the productivity problem in American manufacturing. Ordering supplies, designing products, and monitoring quality control now account for more than 70 percent of the cost of manufacturing a product. Expert systems could take over many of these tasks.

2. Expert systems can be used to train neural networks; neural networks can formulate sensor data into a form that can be used by an expert system; expert systems can control the flow of information through neural networks; and expert systems can analyze responses provided by neural networks.

3. Expert systems are used to recommend strategies, diagnose illness, analyze structures, and train personnel in such fields as law, medicine, engineering, business, geology, financial analysis, and tax analysis.

4. An expert system shell can be purchased as an application software package. Expert system shells offer expert systems technology to people who do not have access to an designer. Expert system shells provide the inference engine, the user interface and the commands of an expert system. The only thing that has to be provided in the domain knowledge.

5. A real-time expert system handles data that is rapidly changing. The input for a real-time system comes from automatic sensors that are monitoring a process rather than from people. The Hubble Space Telescope uses a real-time expert system to help control its complex computer system.

Section VI
Graphical User Interface and Windows 3.0

❑ TRUE/FALSE

1. F   2. F   3. T   4. T   5. T

❑ MATCHING

1. a   2. c   3. a   4. b   5. d

❑ SHORT ANSWER

1. The statement "all applications running under Windows have a standard user interface means that the basics of how to use every Windows application is the same. How to open files, how to copy data, how to cut and paste data, how to print, is the same in all Windows applications, thus simplifying the process of learning how to use application programs.

2. The statement "Windows 3.0 eliminates the 640K barrier for DOS means that Windows can make full use of the extended memory in 286- and 386-based PCs.

3. Other GUIs include Ensemble and Amiga's Workbench. GUIs for Unix systems include Open Look and Motif. NextStep is the GUI for the Next computer.

4. The Program Manager, the Control Panel, and the File Manager are the three major parts of Windows.

5. The four elements of GUI are windows, icons, menus, and a pointing device.

BASIC SUPPLEMENT

Section I
Introduction to BASIC

❏ WORKSHEET

1.

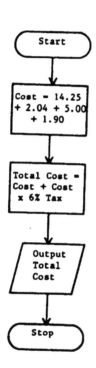

3.

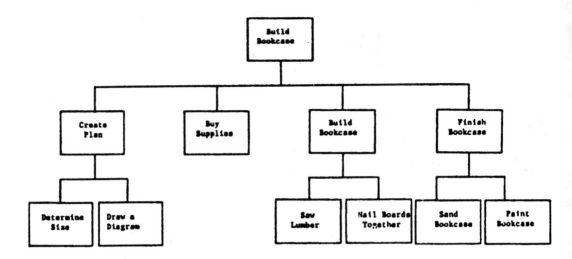

5. a. LIST
    b. LIST 150-200
    c. LIST 20

Section II
BASIC Fundamentals

❏ WORKSHEET

1. c. Character strings must be in double quotation marks.
    d. No embedded commas in numeric constants.

3. a. 8$ — Variable name cannot start with a digit. Valid — N8$.
    b. $X — Variable name must start with a letter. Valid — X$.
    d. F 7 — Variable names may not contain blanks. Valid — F7.

5. a. 5
    b. 27
    c. 37

7. a. Invalid — character strings must be assigned to character string variables.
    b. Invalid — should be: 30 LET X = 3.895

```
10   REM ***              AUTO PARTS INVENTORY           ***
20   REM *** THIS PROGRAM LISTS THE NUMBER OF EACH TYPE  ***
30   REM *** OF PART IN THE INVENTORY AND THE NUMBER     ***
40   REM *** THAT ARE GOOD AND THE NUMBER THAT ARE DEFEC- ***
50   REM *** TIVE.                                        ***
60   REM *** MAJOR VARIABLES:                             ***
70   REM ***     SPK      SPARK PLUGS                     ***
80   REM ***     GSKT     GASKETS                         ***
90   REM ***     BTRY     BATTERIES                       ***
100  REM
110  LET SPK = 7500
120  LET GSKT = 10000
130  LET BTRY = 300
140  REM *** PRINT HEADINGS. ***
150  PRINT "PART","GOOD","DEFECTIVE","TOTAL"
160  PRINT "_____"
170  PRINT "SPARK PLUGS",SPK - (SPK * .12),SPK - (SPK * .88),SPK
180  PRINT "GASKETS",GSKT - (GSKT * .10),GSKT - (GSKT * .90),GSKT
190  PRINT "BATTERIES",BTRY - (BTRY * .075),BTRY - (BTRY * .925),BTRY
999  END
```

PART	GOOD	DEFECTIVE	TOTAL
SPARK PLUGS	6600	900.0001	7500
GASKETS	9000	1000	10000
BATTERIES	277.5	22.5	300

Section III
Input and Output

❏ **WORKSHEET**

1. OWED $ 13.4

3. The READ/DATA statement has the advantage that the data does not have to be entered each time
    the program is executed.

5. a. `10 PRINT "NAME","I.D. NUMBER","OCCUPATION"`

   b. `20 PRINT X;Y;Z$`

      `WHERE IS C?`

   d. `40 PRINT "THE DATE IS";D$`

7.
```
10 LET C$ = "CHAIRS"
20 LET N1 = 8
30 LET T$ = "TABLES"
40 LET N2 = 2

10 READ C$,N1,T$,N2
20 DATA "CHAIRS",8,"TABLES",2

10 INPUT "ENTER FIRST ITEM AND QUANTITY";C$,N1
20 INPUT "ENTER SECOND ITEM AND QUANTITY";T$,N2
```

❑ PROGRAMMING PROBLEM 1

```
10  REM ***                 QUIT SMOKING                    ***
20  REM
30  REM ***   THIS PROGRAM CALCULATES HOW MUCH MONEY BOB & JIM ***
40  REM ***   WILL SAVE PER WEEK & PER YEAR IF THEY GIVE UP    ***
50  REM ***   SMOKING. THE RESULTS DEPEND ON THE COST PER PACK ***
60  REM ***   AND HOW MUCH THEY SMOKE PER DAY.                 ***
70  REM ***   MAJOR VARIABLES:                                 ***
80  REM ***      PACKS      # OF PACKS SMOKED PER DAY          ***
90  REM ***      CST        PRICE OF A PACK OF CIGARETTES      ***
100 REM ***      NME$       NAME OF SMOKER                     ***
110 REM ***      YEAR       MONEY SAVED IN A YEAR              ***
120 REM ***      WEEK       MONEY SAVED IN A WEEK              ***
130 REM
140 REM *** INPUT DATA FOR BOB. ***
150 INPUT "ENTER SMOKER'S NAME "; BNME$
160 INPUT "PACKS SMOKED PER DAY "; BPACK
170 INPUT "PRICE PER PACK "; BCST
180 REM
190 REM *** DETERMINE AMOUNT SAVED PER WEEK AND PER YEAR. ***
200 LET BWEEK = 7 * BPACK * BCST
210 LET BYEAR = 52 * BWEEK
220 REM
230 REM *** INPUT DATA FOR JOE. ***
240 INPUT "ENTER SMOKER'S NAME "; JNME$
250 INPUT "PACKS SMOKED PER DAY "; JPACK
260 INPUT "PRICE PER PACK "; JCST
270 REM
280 REM *** DETERMINE AMOUNT SAVED PER WEEK AND PER YEAR. ***
```

```
290 LET JWEEK = 7 * JPACK * JCST
300 LET JYEAR = 52 * JWEEK
310 REM
320 REM *** PRINT HEADINGS. ***
330 PRINT
340 PRINT "SMOKER'S", "NO. PACKS", "COST", "AMT. SAVED", "AMT. SAVED"
350 PRINT "NAME", "PER DAY", "PER PACK", "PER WEEK", "PER YEAR"
360 PRINT "--------", "---------", "--------", "----------", "----------"
370 REM
380 REM *** PRINT RESULTS. ***
390 PRINT
400 PRINT BNME$, BPACK, BCST, BWEEK, BYEAR
410 PRINT JNME$, JPACK, JCST, JWEEK, JYEAR
999 END

ENTER SMOKER'S NAME ? BOB

PACKS SMOKED PER DAY ? 1.5

PRICE PER PACK ? 2.05

ENTER SMOKER'S NAME ? JIM

PACKS SMOKED PER DAY ? .5

PRICE PER PACK ? 2.20
```

SMOKER'S NAME	NO. PACKS PER DAY	COST PER PACK	AMT. SAVED PER WEEK	AMT. SAVED PER YEAR
BOB	1.5	2.05	21.525	1119.3
JIM	.5	2.2	7.7	400.4

Section IV
The Decision Statement and Functions

☐ WORKSHEET

1. a. 10 IF N$ = "LAST" THEN 99
   b. 20 IF X > 2 THEN PRINT X

3.

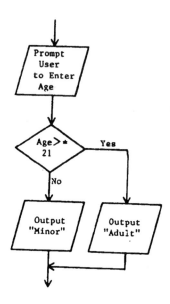

5. 10 IF SD1 = SD2 THEN PRINT "Box is a Square"
   ELSE PRINT "Box is a Rectangle"

7. 10 INPUT "ENTER A CHARACTER STRING";S$
   20 PRINT "THE LENGTH OF THE STRING IS ";LEN(S$)

9. The VAL function can be used to convert a character string value to its numeric equivalent.

❏ PROGRAMMING PROBLEM 1

```
10  REM ***              SHOE STOCK NUMBERS              ***
20  REM
30  REM *** THIS PROGRAM READS A STOCK NUMBERS AND PRINTS   ***
40  REM *** A MESSAGE STATING WHETHER IT IS VALID.          ***
50  REM *** MAJOR VARIABLES:                                ***
60  REM ***    STOCK$              STOCK NUMBER             ***
70  REM ***    LAST$               STRING OF DECIMAL PORTION ***
80  REM ***    PRE$                STRING OF MIDDLE PORTION ***
90  REM ***    LAST                NUMERIC VALUE OF DECIMAL ***
100 REM ***    SUM                 NUMERIC VALUE OF MIDDLE  ***
110 REM
120 REM *** READ THE STOCK NUMBER AND SEPARATE NEEDED NUMBERS. ***
```

```
130 LET SUM = 0
140 INPUT "ENTER THE STOCK NUMBER ";STOCK$
150 LAST$ = RIGHT$(STOCK$,7)
160 PRE$ = MID$(STOCK$,3,3)
170 REM
180 REM *** CONVERT STRING TO NUMERIC EQUIVALENT, COMPUTE SUM. ***
190 LAST = VAL(LAST$)
200 FOR I = 1 TO 3
210    SUM = VAL(MID$(PRE$,I,1)) + SUM
220 NEXT I
230 IF LAST <> SUM THEN PRINT STOCK$;" IS AN INVALID STOCK NUMBER."
       ELSE PRINT STOCK$;" IS A VALID STOCK NUMBER."
999 END

ENTER THE STOCK NUMBER ? QB371.11
QB371.11 IS A VALID STOCK NUMBER.
```

Section V
Looping

❏ WORKSHEET

1. a. 24
   b. 8
   c. -2
   d. 22

3. a. 1   5   9   13   17
   b. 9   10
       6   7
       3   4
       0   1
       -3   -2
   c. Nothing

5. a

7. a. 15 times
   b. 36 times

```
9.  10 FOR ITM = 6 TO 1 STEP -1
    20      READ T$,Q
    30 NEXT ITM
    40 DATA "HAMMER",24,"PLIERS",12
    50 DATA "CHISEL",8,"DRILL",18
    60 DATA "WRENCH",20,"SCREW DRIVER",42
```

❏ PROGRAMMING PROBLEM 1

```
10   REM ***                A PAY RAISE                  ***
20   REM
30   REM *** THIS PROGRAM PRINTS A TABLE OF THE ADDITIONAL   ***
40   REM *** MONEY TO BE PAID ON SALARIES BETWEEN $12-18000. ***
50   REM *** THE PAY HIKE TO BE TESTED IS 4%, 4.5%, AND 5%.  ***
60   REM *** MAJOR VARIABLES:                                ***
70   REM ***     FOUR          4% INCREASE ADDITIONAL PAY    ***
80   REM ***     HALF          4.5% INCREASE ADDITIONAL PAY  ***
90   REM ***     FIVE          5% INCREASE ADDITIONAL PAY    ***
100  REM
110  REM *** PRINT THE HEADINGS. ***
120  PRINT
130  PRINT " SALARY"," +4%"," +4.5%"," +5%"
140  PRINT
150  REM
160  REM *** CALCULATE ADDITIONAL PAY, PRINT IT. ***
170  FOR I = 12000 TO 18000 STEP 1000
180     FOUR = I * .04 + I
190     HALF = I * .045 + I
200     FIVE = I * .05 + I
210     PRINT I,FOUR,HALF,FIVE
220  NEXT I
999  END
```

SALARY	+4%	+4.5%	+5%
12000	12480	12540	12600
13000	13520	13585	13650
14000	14560	14630	14700

```
15000          15600          15675          15750
16000          16640          16720          16800
17000          17680          17765          17850
18000          18720          18810          18900
```

Section VI
Modularizing Programs

❏ WORKSHEET

1. Control is transferred depending on the value of the stated expression. If the expression evaluates as 1, control is transferred to the first subroutine listed, if it evaluates as 2, control is transferred to the second subroutine, and so forth.

3. The ON/GOSUB expression must be numeric.

5. The subroutine is missing a RETURN statement.

7. `350 ON (X /3 - 1) GOSUB 9000, 2000, 3000`

9.
```
1000 REM *** CHECKS FOR INVALID ACCOUNT NUMBER. ***
1010 INPUT "ENTER ACCOUNT NUMBER (1-999)";ACCTNUM
1020 WHILE (ACCTNUM < 1) OR (ACCTNUM > 999)
1030    PRINT "PLEASE REENTER THE ACCOUNT NUMBER."
1040    INPUT "IT MUST BE FROM 1 - 999";ACCTNUM
1050 NEXT
```

❏ PROGRAMMING PROBLEM 1

```
10   REM ***                PROGRAM BOOKCOST            ***
20   REM
30   REM *** THIS PROGRAM CALCULATES THE TOTAL COST OF A   ***
40   REM *** BOOK.  THE TOTAL COST IS OBTAINED BY ADDING   ***
50   REM *** THE PRICE OF THE BOOK TO THE PROCESSING COST, ***
60   REM *** WHICH IS BASED ON THE TYPE.                   ***
70   REM ***    1.  REFERENCE BOOK                         ***
80   REM ***           NOT A DUPLICATE    $8.50            ***
90   REM ***           DUPLICATE          $7.40            ***
100  REM ***    2.  CIRCULATING BOOK                       ***
110  REM ***           NOT A DUPLICATE    $7.82            ***
120  REM ***           DUPLICATE          $6.60            ***
140  REM ***    3.  PAPERBACK                              ***
```

```
150  REM ***            NOT A DUPLICATE    $4.60         ***
160  REM ***            DUPLICATE          $3.10         ***
170  REM
180  REM *** MAJOR VARIABLES:                            ***
190  REM ***    PRICE     PRICE OF THE BOOK              ***
200  REM ***    CODE      TYPE OF BOOK AS ABOVE          ***
210  REM ***    DUP$      IS BOOK A DUPLICATE(Y/N)?      ***
220  REM ***    PRCST     PROCESSING COST                ***
230  REM ***    TTCST     TOTAL COST OF BOOK             ***
240  REM
250  REM *** CALL SUBROUTINE TO ENTER DATA.             ***
260  GOSUB 1000
270  REM
280  REM *** CALL APPROPRIATE SUBROUTINE TO CALCULATE.  ***
290  REM *** THE PROCESSING COST.                       ***
300  ON CODE GOSUB 2000, 3000, 4000
310  REM
320  REM *** CALL SUBROUTINE TO ADD PROCESSING COST TO  ***
330  REM *** BOOK PRICE AND PRINT TOTAL COST.           ***
340  GOSUB 5000
350  GOTO 9999
1000 REM ******************************************************
1010 REM ***            SUBROUTINE ENTER DATA           ***
1020 REM ******************************************************
1030 REM *** SUBROUTINE TO ALLOW USER TO ENTER DATA.    ***
1040 REM
1050 CLS
1060 INPUT "ENTER PRICE OF THE BOOK"; PRICE
1070 PRINT
1080 PRINT "1 - REFERENCE BOOK"
1090 PRINT "2 - CIRCULATING BOOK"
1100 PRINT "3 - PAPERBACK"
1110 INPUT "ENTER TYPE CODE FOR THE BOOK, USING THE CODE LISTED ABOVE"; CODE
1120 PRINT
1130 INPUT "IS BOOK A DUPLICATE (Y/N)"; DUP$
1140 RETURN
2000 REM ******************************************************
2010 REM ***            SUBROUTINE REFERENCE BOOK       ***
2020 REM ******************************************************
2030 REM *** SUBROUTINE TO CALCULATE PROCESSING COST OF ***
2040 REM *** REFERENCE BOOK.                            ***
2050 REM
2060 IF DUP$ = "Y" THEN PRCST = 7.4 ELSE PRCST = 8.5
2070 RETURN
3000 REM ******************************************************
3010 REM ***            SUBROUTINE CIRCULATING BOOK     ***
```

```
3020 REM ******************************************************
3030 REM *** SUBROUTINE TO CALCULATE PROCESSING COST OF     ***
3040 REM *** CIRCULATING BOOK.                              ***
3050 REM
3060 IF DUP$ = "Y" THEN PRCST = 6.6 ELSE PRCST = 7.82
3090 RETURN
4000 REM ******************************************************
4010 REM ***           SUBROUTINE PAPERBACK BOOK            ***
4020 REM ******************************************************
4030 REM *** SUBROUTINE TO CALCULATE PROCESSING COST OF     ***
4040 REM *** PAPERBACK BOOK.                                ***
4050 REM
4060 IF DUP$ = "Y" THEN PRCST = 3.1 ELSE PRCST = 4.6
4070 RETURN
5000 REM ******************************************************
5010 REM ***              SUBROUTINE PRINT COST             ***
5020 REM ******************************************************
5030 REM *** SUBROUTINE TO CALCULATE AND PRINT TOTAL COST. ***
5040 REM
5050 TTCST = PRCST + PRICE
5060 PRINT USING "\                      \ $$###.##"; "*** TOTAL COST:"; TTCST
5070 RETURN
9999 END


ENTER PRICE OF THE BOOK? 24.75


1 - REFERENCE BOOK
2 - CIRCULATING BOOK
3 - PAPERBACK
ENTER TYPE CODE FOR THE BOOK, USING THE CODE LISTED ABOVE? 3
IS BOOK A DUPLICATE (Y/N)? N


*** TOTAL COST:        $29.35
```

Section VII
Arrays

❑ WORKSHEET

1. a. 125
   b. 1
   c. 75

d. 16

e. 1

f. 100

3. 80 DIM N(99)

5. 100

7.

```
 7    9   22    1
36    5   11    6
12   32   10   49
```

9.

```
250 FOR I = 1 TO 3
260    FOR J = 1 TO 5
270       R(I) = R(I) + G(I,J)
280    NEXT J
290 NEXT I
```

❑ PROGRAMMING PROBLEM 1

```
10    REM ***                    GROCERY STORE WARS              ***
20
30    REM *** THIS PROGRAM PRINTS A REPORT OF LOCAL PRICES AND   ***
40    REM *** DETERMINES THE STORE WITH THE OVERALL BEST PRICES  ***
50    REM *** FOR FOUR GIVEN STORES.                             ***
60    REM *** MAJOR VARIABLES:                                   ***
70    REM ***    NAM$              NAME OF THE STORE             ***
80    REM ***    PRICE             PRICE OF EACH ITEM            ***
90    REM ***    TTAL              TOTAL FOR EACH STORE          ***
100   REM ***    FLAG, H, H$       SORT VARIABLES
110   REM
120   DIM NAM$(4), PRICE(4,3), TTAL(4)
130   REM
140   REM *** READ PRICES. ***
150   GOSUB 1000
160   REM *** COMPUTE TOTAL PRICE. ***
170   GOSUB 2000
180   REM *** PRINT STORE AND PRICES. ***
190   GOSUB 3000
200 REM *** COMPUTE AND PRINT WINNER. ***
210 GOSUB 4000
220 GOTO 9999
1000 REM ***********************************************
```

```
1010 REM ***              SUBROUTINE READ              ***
1020 REM ***********************************************
1030 REM
1040 FOR I = 1 TO 4
1050    READ NAM$(I)
1060    FOR J = 1 TO 3
1070       READ PRICE(I,J)
1080    NEXT J
1090 NEXT I
1100 RETURN
2000 REM ***********************************************
2010 REM ***              SUBROUTINE TOTALS            ***
2020 REM ***********************************************
2030 REM
2040 FOR I = 1 TO 4
2050    FOR J = 1 TO 3
2060       TTAL(I) = TTAL(I) + PRICE(I,J)
2070    NEXT J
2080 NEXT I
2090 RETURN
3000 REM ***********************************************
3010 REM ***              SUBROUTINE PRINT             ***
3020 REM ***********************************************
3030 REM
3040 REM *** PRINT REPORT HEADINGS. ***
3050 PRINT TAB(22);"THE GREAT GROCERY WAR"
3060 PRINT
3070 PRINT TAB(23);"PRICE PER";TAB(41);"PRICE PER";TAB(55);"PRICE PER"
3080 PRINT TAB(4);"STORE";TAB(21);"LB HAMBURGER";TAB(39);"HEAD/LETTUCE";
3090 PRINT TAB(53);"LOAF OF BREAD"
3100 PRINT
3110 FOR I = 1 TO 4
3120    PRINT NAM$(I);TAB(24);
3130    FOR J = 1 TO 3
3140       PRINT PRICE(I,J),
3150    NEXT J
3160    PRINT
3170 NEXT I
3180 RETURN
4000 REM ***********************************************
4010 REM ***              SUBROUTINE SORT              ***
4020 REM ***********************************************
4030 REM
4040 FLAG = 0
4050 FOR I = 1 TO 3
4060    IF TTAL(I) <= TTAL(I + 1) THEN 4120
```

```
4070      H = TTAL(I)
4080      H$ = NAM$(I)
4081      TTAL(I) = TTAL(I + 1)
4082      NAM$(I) = NAM$(I + 1)
4090      TTAL(I + 1) = H
4100      NAM$(I + 1) = H$
4110      FLAG = 1
4120 NEXT I
4130 IF FLAG = 1 THEN 4040
4140 REM
4150 REM *** PRINT THE WINNER. ***
4160 PRINT "THE WINNER OF THE GROCERY WARS CONTEST IS "; NAM$(1)
4170 RETURN
4180 REM
4190 REM *** DATA STATEMENTS ***
4200 DATA "KATHY'S SUPERMARKET",1.08,0.99,0.35
4210 DATA "KEY FOOD",1.11,0.89,0.40
4220 DATA "CHURCH'S",0.99,0.99,0.38
4230 DATA "THE MARKET PLACE",1.18,0.89,0.40
9999 END
```

THE GREAT GROCERY WAR

STORE	PRICE PER LB HAMBURGER	PRICE PER HEAD/LETTUCE	PRICE PER LOAF OF BREAD
KATHY'S SUPERMARKET	1.08	.99	.35
KEY FOOD	1.11	.89	.4
CHURCH'S	.99	.99	.38
THE MARKET PLACE	1.18	.89	.4

THE WINNER OF THE GROCERY WARS CONTEST IS CHURCHS